THE SAXONS IN BRITAIN

THE SAXONS IN BRITAIN

THOMAS MILLER

THE SAXONS IN BRITAIN

THOMAS MILLER

First published in Great Britain by David Bogue, London, 1850, as part of the title *History of the Anglo-Saxons*.

This edition © 2020 A Distant Mirror

ISBN 9780648870517

A DISTANT MIRROR

 adistantmirror.com

 admin@adistantmirror.com

contents

BEFORE THE SAXONS

1. The Dawn of History — 9
2. The Ancient Britons — 19
3. The Druids — 31
4. Landing of Julius Cæsar — 39
5. Caractacus, Boadicea, and Agricola — 59
6. Departure of the Romans — 77
7. Britain after the Roman Period — 92

THE SAXON INVASION

8. The Ancient Saxons — 105
9. Hengist, Horsa, Rowena, and Vortigern — 117
10. Ella, Cerdric, and King Arthur — 131
11. Establishment of the Saxon Octarchy — 147
12. The Conversion of Ethelbert — 159
13. Edwin, King of the Deiri and Bernicia — 171
14. Penda, the Pagan Monarch of Mercia — 189
15. Decline of the Saxon Octarchy — 202
16. Offa the Terrible — 217
17. Egbert, King of All the Saxons — 233

APPENDICES

ANGLO-SAXON CULTURE

Religion — 242
Government and Laws — 250
Literature — 257
Architecture, Art, & Science — 264
Costume, Manners, Customs, and Everyday Life — 272

BEFORE THE SAXONS

1 The Dawn of History

> This fortress, built by Nature for herself
> Against infection and the hand of war,
> This earth of majesty – this little world –
> This precious stone set in the silver sea –
> England, bound in with the triumphant sea,
> Whose rocky shore beats back the envious surge
> Of watery Neptune.
>
> – *Shakespeare*

ALMOST EVERY HISTORIAN regrets how little is known of the early inhabitants of Great Britain – a fact which all lovers of antiquity can deplore, since among all we can with certainty glean from the pages of contemporary history, we can find little more than if we possessed written records of the remotest origin of the American Indians; for both would alike be the history of an unlettered and largely unknown race.

The same obscurity, with scarcely an exception, hangs over the primeval inhabitants of every other country. If we lift the mysterious curtain which has so long fallen over and concealed the past, we obtain glimpses only of obscure hieroglyphics; and from the fables of monsters and giants, to which all nations trace their origin, we glance backward and backward, to find that Rome and Greece can produce no better authorities than old undated traditions, teeming with fabulous accounts of gods and goddesses.

What we can see of the remote past through the twilight of time is like a great and unknown sea, on which some solitary ship is afloat, whose course we cannot trace through the shadows which everywhere deepen around her; nor can we tell what strange land

lies beyond the dim horizon to which she seems bound.

The dark night of mystery has forever settled down upon the early history of our island, and the first dawn which throws the shadow of man upon the scene reveals a rude hunter, clad in the skins of beasts, whose path is disputed by the maned and shaggy bison, whose rude hut in the forest is pitched beside the lair of the hungry wolf, and whose first conquest is found among these formidable animals.

And so, in as few words, might the early history of many a country or race be written.

The shores of Time are strewn with the remains of extinct animals, which, when living, the eye of man never looked upon – as if from the deep sea of Eternity a great wave had heaved up, which washed over and blotted out forever all that was coeval with her silent and ancient reign, leaving a monument upon the confines of this old and obliterated world, for man in a far and future day to read, and on which stands engraved the solemn words: *This far you shall come, but no further – beyond this boundary all is Mine!*

Neither does this mystery end here, for around the monuments

which were raised by the earliest inhabitants of Great Britain, there still reigns a deep darkness. We have no idea what hand piled together the rude remains of Stonehenge; and we have very few records of the manners, the customs, or the religion of the early Britons. Here and there a colossal barrow heaves up above the dead; we look within, and find a few bones, a few rude weapons, either used in war or the chase, and these are all. And we gaze in wonder at such remains.

Who those ancient voyagers were that first called England 'the country of sea cliffs', we do not know; and while we sit and brood over the rude fragments of the Welsh Triads, we become so entangled in doubt and mystery as to look upon the son of Aedd the Great, and the Island of Honey to which he sailed, and wherein he found no man alive, as the pleasing dream of some old and forgotten poet; and we set out again, with no more success, to

---

1. The Welsh Triads (Welsh: *Trioedd Ynys Prydein*) are a group of related texts in medieval manuscripts which preserve fragments of Welsh folklore, mythology and traditional history in groups of three. The triad is a rhetorical form whereby objects are grouped together in threes, with a heading indicating the point of likeness; for example "Three things not easily restrained, the flow of a torrent, the flight of an arrow, and the tongue of a fool." The texts include references to King Arthur and other semi-historical characters.

discover who were the earliest inhabitants of England, leaving the ancient Cymri and the country of Summer behind, and the tall, silent cliffs, to stand as they had done for ages, looking over a wide and mastless sea.

We then look among the ancient names of the headlands, and harbours, and mountains, and hills, and valleys, and endeavour to trace any resemblance to a language spoken by some neighbouring nation, and we find only a few scattered words, which leave us still in doubt, like a confusion of echoes, one breaking in upon the other – a mixture of Celtic, Pictish, Gaulish, and Saxon sounds, where if for a moment one is audible and distinct, it is soon drowned by other successive clamours which come panting up with a still louder claim, and eventually, in despair, we are compelled to step back again into the old primeval silence.

There we find Geology looking daringly into the formation of the early world, and boldly proclaiming that there was a period of time when our island heaved up bare and desolate amid the silence of the surrounding ocean – when on its ancient promontories and grey granite peaks not a green branch waved, nor a blade of grass grew, and no living thing, saving the tiny corals, as they piled dome upon dome above the naked foundations of this early world, stirred in the 'deep profound' which reigned over those sleeping seas.

Onward they go, boldly discoursing of undated centuries that have passed away, during which they tell us the ocean swarmed with huge, monstrous forms; and that all those countless ages have left to record their flight are but the remains of a few extinct reptiles and fishes, whose living likenesses never again appeared in the world.

Then to another measureless period are we fearlessly carried – so long as to be numbered only in the account of Time which Eternity keeps – and other forms, we are told, moved over the floors of dried-up oceans – vast animals which no human eye ever looked upon alive; these, they say, also were swept away, and their ponderous remains had long mingled with and enriched the earth; but man had not as yet appeared; nor in any corner of the whole wide world do we discover in the deep-buried layers of the earth even a single vestige of the remains of the human race.

*

What historian, then, with such facts as these before him, will not hesitate before identifying the first inhabitants of any country, where they came from, or at what period that country was first inhabited? The historian might as well attempt a description of the scenery over which the mornings of the early world first broke – of summits and peaks which ages ago have been hurled down, and ground and powdered into dust.

Of what importance is the date when such things were, or at what time or place they first appeared? We can gaze upon the gigantic remains of the mastodon or mammoth, or on the grey, silent ruins of Stonehenge, but at what period of time the one roamed over our island, or in what year the other was first reared, will for ever remain a mystery.

The earth beneath our feet is full of proofs that there was an age in which these extinct monsters existed, and that period is empty

of any evidence of the existence of man on our island. And during those periods when oceans were emptied and dried up, amid the heaving up and burying of rocks and mountains – when volcanoes reddened the dark midnights of the world, when 'the earth was without form, and void' and the Spirit 'moved upon the face of the waters' – what mortal eye might have looked upon the rocking and reeling of those chaotic ruins when their rude forms first heaved up into the light?

Is not such a world stamped with the imprint of the Omnipotent, from when He first paved its foundation with enduring granite, and roofed it over with the soft blue of heaven, and lighted it by day with the glorious sun, and hung out the moon and stars to gladden the night – until at last He fashioned a world beautiful enough for the abode of His own image to dwell in – all before He created man?

And what does it matter whether or not we believe in all these mighty epochs? Surely it is enough for us to discover throughout every change of time the loving-kindness of God for mankind; we see how fitting this globe was at last for his dwelling place; that before the Great Architect had put this last finish to His mighty

work, instead of leaving us to starve amid the Silurian sterility, He prepared the world for man, and in place of the naked granite, spread out a rich carpet of verdure for him to tread upon, then flung upon it a profusion of the sweetest flowers.

Let us not, then, say 'thus it was fashioned', and 'so it was formed', but with our silence acknowledge that it has never yet entered into the heart or mind of man to understand how the Almighty Creator laid the foundation of the world.

To His great works we must come with reverential knee, and bow before them; for the grey rocks, and the high mountain summits, and the wide-spreading plains, and the ever-sounding seas, are stamped with the image of Eternity – a mighty shadow hangs over them. The grey and weather-beaten headlands still look over the sea, and the solemn mountains still slumber under their old midnight shadows – but what human ear first heard the murmur of the waves upon the beach; or what human foot first climbed those high-piled summits? We can never know.

What would it help us if we knew the date when our island was buried beneath the ocean? Or when what was dry land in one age became the sea in another? When volcanoes glowed angrily under the dark skies of the early world, and huge extinct monsters bellowed, and roamed and swam through the old forests and the ancient rivers which have perhaps ages ago been swept away? What could we find more to interest us were we in possession of the names, the ages, and the numbers, of the first adventurers who were perchance driven by some storm upon our sea-beaten coast, than what is said in the ancient Triad before alluded to –

"There were no more men alive, nor anything but bears,
  wolves, beavers, and the oxen with the high prominence..."

when Aedd landed upon the shores of England.

What few traces we have of the religious rites of the early inhabitants of Britain vary little from those that have been seen by modern travellers who have visited newly-discovered countries in our own age.

We have yet to learn by what hands the round towers of Ireland were raised, and by what race the few ancient British monuments that still remain were piled together. We cannot enter those mysterious gates which open upon the true History of the Past.

We find the footprint of man there, but who he was, or from where he came, we do not know. He lived and died, and whether or not history would ever remember the monuments he left behind did not concern him. Whether the stones would mark the temple in which he worshipped, or tumble down and cover his grave, did not concern him. With his stone axe, and spear-head of flint, he hewed his way from the cradle to the tomb, and under the steep barrow he knew that he should sleep his last sleep – and with his arms folded upon his breast, he left the past to bury its dead.

He did not live for us.

Aborigines of England

2 THE ANCIENT BRITONS

> Where the maned bison and the wolf did roam,
> The ancient Briton reared his wattled home,
> Paddled his coracle across the mere,
> In the dim forest chased the antlered deer;
> Pastured his herds within the open glade,
> Played with his 'young barbarians' in the shade;
> And when the new moon o'er the high hills broke,
> Worshipped his heathen gods
> beneath the sacred oak.
>
> – *The Old Forest*

Although the origin of the early inhabitants of Great Britain is still open to many doubts, we have good evidence that in the remote past the descendants of the ancient Cimmerii, or Cymry, dwelt in Britain, and that from the same great family sprang the Celtic tribe; a portion of which at that early period inhabited the opposite coast of France.

At what time the Cymry and Celts first peopled England we have no written record, though there is evidence that they were known to the early Phœnician voyagers many centuries before the Roman invasion, and that the ancient Greeks were acquainted with the British Islands by the name of the Cassiterides, or the 'Islands of Tin'.

Thus both the Greeks and Romans indirectly traded with the very race whose ancestors had shaken the imperial city with their arms, and brought the tide of battle close to the shores of Greece.

They were the undoubted offspring of the dark Cimmerii of antiquity, those dreaded inhabitants of caves and forests, whose formidable helmets were surmounted by the figures of gaping and hideous monsters; who wore high crests to make them look taller

and more terrible in battle, and who considered death in battle as the crowning triumph of all earthly glory.

From this race sprang those ancient British tribes who presented a bold front to Julius Cæsar, when his Roman galleys first ploughed the waves that washed their storm-beaten shores.

Beyond this, history has nothing for us; and the Welsh traditions go no further back than to state that when the son of Aedd first sailed over the ocean, the island was uninhabited – which we may take to mean that the portion on which he and his followers landed was empty, for it seems unlikely that Britain would have been entirely empty, visible as it is on a clear day from the opposite coast of Gaul, and beyond which great nations had for centuries flourished.

What few records we possess of the ancient Britons reveal a wild and hardy race. They had their chiefs and rulers who wore armour, and ornaments of gold and silver; and these held in subjection the poorer races who lived upon the produce of the chase, the wild fruits and roots which the forest and the field produced, and wore skins, and dwelt in caverns which they hewed out of the old grey rocks.

They were priest-ridden by the ancient druids, who cursed and excommunicated without the aid of either bell, book, or candle. They burned and slaughtered all unbelievers just as well as

Mahomet does, or the bigoted fanatics who in later times would perform the same deeds under the mask of the Romish religion.

For centuries after, mankind had not undergone so great a change as they at the first appear to have done; there was the same love of power, the same shedding of blood, and those who had not courage to take the field openly and seize upon what they could boldly, burnt, and slew, and sacrificed their fellow-men under the plea that such offerings were acceptable to the gods.

By the aid of the few hints which are scattered over the works of the Greek and Roman writers, the existence of a few remaining monuments, and the discoveries which have many a time been made through numberless excavations, we can just make out, in the hazy evening of the past, enough of the dim forms of the ancient Britons to see their mode of life, their habits in peace and war, as they move about in the twilight shadows which have settled down over two thousand years.

That they were a tall and muscular race, we have the authority of the Roman writers to prove; who, however, add but little in praise of the symmetry of their figures, though they were near half a foot higher than their distant kindred the Gauls. They wore their hair long and thrown back from the forehead, which must have given them a wild look in the excitement of battle, when their long curling locks would heave and fall with every blow they struck; the upper lip of the males was unshaven, and

the long tufts drooped over the mouth, thus adding greatly to their grim and warlike appearance. Added to this, they cast aside their upper garments when they fought, as the brave Highlanders were wont to do a century or two ago, and on their naked bodies were punctured all kinds of monsters, such as no human eye had ever beheld. Claudian mentions the "fading figures on the dying Pict"

– the dim deathly blue that they would fade into, as the life-blood of the rude warrior ebbed out upon the field of battle.

How different must have been the landscape which the fading rays of the evening sunset gilded in that rude and primitive age. Instead of the tall towers and walled

cities, whose glittering windows now flash back the golden light, the sinking rays gilded a barrier of felled trees in the centre of the forest which surrounded the wattled and thatched huts of those ancient herdsmen, throwing its crimson rays upon the clear space behind, in which his herds and flocks were pastured for the night; while all around heaved up the grand and gloomy old forest, with its shadowy thickets, and dark dingles, and woody valleys untrodden by the foot of man.

There was then the dreaded wolf to guard against, the unexpected rush of the wild boar, the growl of the grizzly bear, and the bellowing of the maned bison to startle him from his slumber. Nor less to be feared was the midnight marauder from some neighbouring tribe, whom neither the dreaded fires of the heathen druids, nor the awful sentence which held accursed all who communicated with him after the doom was uttered, could keep from plunder, whenever an opportunity presented itself. The subterranean chambers in which their corn was stored might be emptied before morning; the wicker basket which contained their salt (brought from far over the distant sea by the

Phœnicians or some adventurous voyager) might be carried away; and no trace of the robber could be found through the pathless forest, and the reedy morass by which he would escape, while he startled the badger with his tread, and drove the beaver into his ancient home; for beside the druids there were those who sowed no grain, who drank up the beverage their neighbours brewed from their own barley, and ate up the curds which they had made from the milk of their own herds.

These were such as dug up the 'pig-nuts,' still eaten by the children in the northern counties at the present day; who struck down the deer, the boar, and the bison in the wild unenclosed forest – kindled a fire with the dried leaves and dead branches, then threw themselves down at the foot of the nearest oak, when their rude repast was over, and with their war-hatchet, or hunting-spear, firmly grasped, even in sleep, awaited the first beam of morning, unless awoke before by the howl of the wolf, or the thundering of the boar through the thicket. They left the fish in their vast rivers untouched, as if they preferred only that food which could be won by danger; from the timid hare they turned away, to give chase to the antlered monarch of the forest; they let the wild goose float upon the lonely mere, and the plumed duck swim about the broad lake undisturbed. There was a wild independence in their forest life – they had but few wants, and where nature no longer supplied these from her own uncultivated stores, they looked abroad and harassed the more civilized and industrious tribes.

Although there is but little doubt that the British chiefs, and those who dwelt on the sea coast, and opened a trade with the Gaulish merchants, lived in a state of comparative luxury, when contrasted with the wilder tribes who inhabited the interior of the island, still there is something simple and primitive in all that we can collect of their domestic habits.

Their seats consisted of three-legged stools, no doubt sawn crossways from the stem of the tree, and three holes made to hold the legs, like the seats which are called 'crickets,' that may be seen in the huts of the English peasantry in the present day. Their beds consisted of dried grass, leaves, or rushes spread upon the floor –

their covering, the dark blue cloak or sagum which they wore out of doors; or the dried skins of the cattle they slew, either from their own herds or in the chase. They ate and drank from off wooden trenchers, and out of bowls rudely hollowed: they were not without a rough kind of red earthenware, badly baked, and roughly formed. They kept their provisions in baskets of wicker-work, and made their boats of the same material, over which they stretched skins to keep out the water. They kindled fires on the floors of their thatched huts, and appear to have been acquainted with the use of coal as fuel, though there is little doubt that they only dug up such as lay near the surface of the earth; but it was from the great forests which covered their island that they principally gathered their fuel.

They had also boats, not unlike the canoes still in use amongst the Indians, which were formed out of the hollow trunk of a tree; and some of which have been found upwards of thirty feet in length; and in these, no doubt, they ventured over to the opposite coast of France, and even Ireland, when the weather was calm.

Diodorus says that amongst the Celtic tribes there was a simplicity of manners very different to that craft and wickedness

which mankind then exhibited – that they were satisfied with frugal sustenance, and avoided the luxuries of wealth. The boundaries of their pastures consisted of such primitive marks as upright stones, reminding us of the patriarchal age and the scriptural anathema of 'cursed is he who removeth his neighbour's land-mark.'

Their costume was similar to that worn by their kindred the Gauls, consisting of loose lower garments, a kind of waistcoat with wide sleeves, and over this a cloak, or sagum, made of cloth or skin; and when of the former, dyed blue or black, for they were acquainted with the art of dyeing; and some of them wore a cloth, chequered with various colours.

The chiefs wore rings of gold, silver, or bronze, on their

forefingers; they had also ornaments, such as bracelets and armlets of the same metal, and a decoration called the torque, which was either a collar or a belt formed of gold, silver, or bronze, and which fastened behind by a strong hook. Several of these ornaments have been discovered, and amongst them, one of gold, which weighed 25 ounces. It seems to have been something like the mailed gorget of a later day, worn above the cuirass or coat of mail, to protect the neck and throat in battle; their shoes appear to have been only a sole of wood or leather, fastened to the foot by thongs cut from off the raw hides of oxen they had slaughtered.

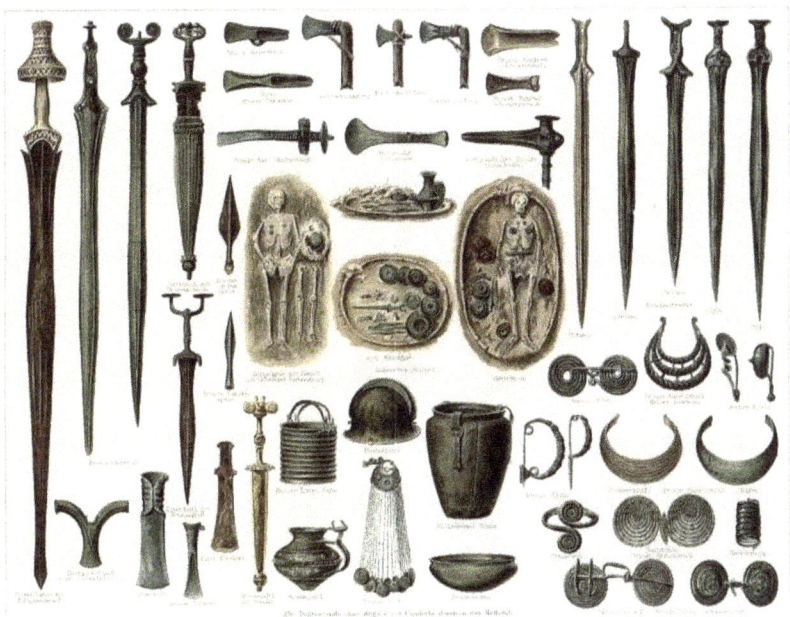

The war weapons of the wilder tribes in the earlier times were hatchets of stone, and arrows headed with flint, and long spears pointed with sharpened bone; but long before the Roman invasion, the more civilized were in possession of battle-axes, swords, spears, javelins, and other formidable instruments of war, made of a mixture of copper and tin. Many of these instruments have been discovered in the ancient barrows where they buried their dead; and were, no doubt, at first procured from the merchants with whom they traded – ignorant, perhaps, for a long

period, that they were produced from the very material they were giving for them in exchange. In battle they also bore a circular shield, coated with the same metal; this they held in the hand by the centre bar that went across the hollow inner space from which the boss projected.

But the war-chariots which they brought into battle were of all things the most dreaded by the Romans. From the axles projected those sharp-hooked formidable scythes, which appalled even the bravest legions, and made such gaps in their well-trained ranks, as struck their boldest generals aghast. These were drawn by such horses as, by their fire and speed, won the admiration of the invaders; for fleet on foot as deer, and with their dark manes streaming out like banners, they rushed headlong, with thundering tramp, into the armed ranks of the enemy; the sharp scythes cutting down every obstacle they came in contact with.

With fixed eyes the fearless warrior hurled his pointed javelins in every direction as he rushed thundering on – sometimes making a thrust with his spear or sword, as he swept by with lightning-speed, or dragged with him for a few yards the affrighted enemy he had grasped while passing, and whose limbs those formidable weapons mangled at every turn until the dreaded

Briton released his hold. Now stepping upon the pole, he aimed a blow at the opponent who attempted to check his speed – then he stopped his quick-footed coursers in a moment, as if a bolt from heaven had alighted, and struck them dead, while some warrior who was watching their onward course fell dead beneath so unexpected a blow; and ere the sword of his companion was uplifted to revenge his death, the Briton and his chariot were far away, hewing a new path through the centre of veteran ranks, which the stormy tide of battle had never before broken.

The form of the tall warrior, leaning over his chariot with glaring eye and clenched teeth, would, by his valour and martial deportment, have done honour to the plains of Troy, and won an immortal line from Homer himself, had he but witnessed those deeds achieved by the British heroes in a later day. What fear of death had they before their eyes who believed that their souls passed at once into the body of some brave warrior, or that they but quitted the battlefield to be admitted into the abodes of the gods?

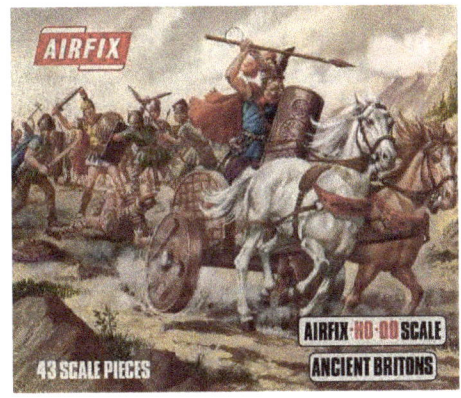

They sprang from a race whose mothers and wives had many a time hemmed in the back of battle, and with their own hands struck down the first of their tribe who fled – sparing neither father, husband, brother, nor son, if he once turned his back upon the enemy: a race whose huge war drums had, centuries before, sounded in Greek and Roman combats.

And to this hardy stock, which drooped awhile beneath the weight of Rome, was the Gothic grandeur of the Saxon stem grafted, and when its antique roots had been manured by the bones of thousands of Danes, and then its exuberant shoots lopped by the swords of the Norman invaders, there sprang up that mighty tree, the shadows of whose branches today stretch far away over the pathless ocean, reaching to the uttermost ends of the earth.

3 THE DRUIDS

> You Druids now maintain
> Your barbarous rites, and sacrifice again;
> You know what heaven is, and gods alone can tell,
> Or else alone are ignorant: you dwell
> In vast and desert woods; you teach no spirit,
> Pluto's pale kingdom can by death inherit:
> They in another world inform again,
> The space betwixt two lives is all the death.
>
> – Lucan's *Pharsalia*

To Julius Cæsar, we are indebted for the clearest description of the religious rites and ceremonies of the Druids; and as he beheld them administered by these priests to the ancient Britons, so they had no doubt existed for several centuries before the Roman invasion, and are therefore matters of history, prior to that period.

There was a wild poetry about their heathenish creed, something gloomy, and grand, and supernatural in the dim, dreamy old forests where their altars were raised: in the deep shadows which hung over their rude grey cromlechs, on which the sacred fire burned. We catch glimpses between the gnarled and twisted stems of those magnificent and aged oaks of the solemn-looking druid, in his white robe of office, his flowing beard blown for a moment aside, and breaking the dark green of the underwood with the lower portion of his sweeping drapery, while he stands like a grave enchanter, his deep sunk and terrible eyes fixed upon the blue smoke as it curls upward amid the foliage – fixed, yet only to appearance; for let but a light and wandering expression pass over one single countenance in that assembled group, and those deep grey piercing eyes would be seen glaring in anger upon the culprit, and whether it were youth or maiden, they would be banished from the sacrifice, and all held accursed who dared to commune with them – a curse more terrible than that which knelled the doom of the excommunicated in a later day.

There were none bold enough to extinguish the baleful fire which was kindled around the wicker idol, when its angry flames went crackling above the heads of the human victims who were offered up to appease their brutal gods. In the centre of their darksome forests were their rich treasures piled together, the plunder of war; the wealth wrested from some neighbouring tribe; rich ornaments brought by unknown voyagers from distant countries in exchange for the tin which the island produced; or trophies won by the British warriors who had fought in the ranks of the Gauls on the opposite shore – all piled without order together, and guarded only by the superstitious dread which they threw around everything they possessed; for there ever hung the fear of a dreadful death over the head of the plunderer who dared to touch the treasures which were allotted to the awful druids.

They kept no written record of their innermost mysteries, but amid the drowsy rustling of the leaves and the melancholy murmuring of the waters which ever flowed around their wooded abodes, they taught the secrets of their cruel creed to those who for long years had aided in the administration of their horrible ceremonies, who without a blanched cheek or a quailing heart had grown grey beneath the blaze of human sacrifices, and fired the wicker pile with an unshaken hand – these alone were the truly initiated.

They left the younger disciples to mumble over matters of less import – written doctrines which taught how the soul passed into other bodies in never-ending succession; but they permitted them not to meddle in matters of life and death; and many came from afar to study a religion which armed the druids with more than sovereign power. All law was administered by the same dreaded priests; no one dared to appeal from their awful decree; he who was once sentenced had but to bow his head and obey – rebellion was death, and a curse was thundered against all who ventured to approach him; from that moment he became an outcast amongst mankind.

To impress the living with a dread of their power even after death, they hesitated not in their doctrines to proclaim that they held control over departed and rebellious souls; and in the midnight winds that went wailing through the shadowy forests, they bade their believers listen to the cry of the disembodied spirits who were moaning for forgiveness, and were driven by every blast that blew against the opening arms of the giant oaks; for they gave substance to shadows, and pointed out forms in the dark-moving clouds to add to the terrors of their creed. They worshipped the sun and moon, and ever kept the sacred fire burning upon some awful altar which had been reddened by the blood of sacrifice.

They headed the solemn processions to springs and fountains, and muttered their incantations over the moving water, for, next to fire, it was the element they held in the highest veneration. But their grand temples – like Stonehenge – stood in the centre of light, in the midst of broad, open, and spacious plains, and there the great Beltian fire was kindled; there the distant tribes congregated together, and unknown gods were evoked, whose

very names have perished, and whose existence could only be found in the wooded hill, the giant tree, or the murmuring spring or fountain, over which they were supposed to preside.

There sat the arch-druid, in his white surplice, the shadow of the mighty pillars of rough-hewn stone chequering the stony rim of that vast circle – from his neck suspended the wonderful egg which his credulous believers said fell from twined serpents, that vanished hissing high in the air, after having in vain pursued the mounted horseman who caught it, then galloped off at full speed – that egg, cased in gold, which could by its magical virtues swim against the stream. He held the mysterious symbol of office, in his hands more potent than the sceptre swayed by the most powerful of monarchs that ever sat upon our island throne, as he sat with his brow furrowed by long thought, and ploughed deep by many a meditated plot, while his soul spurned the ignorant herd who were assembled around him, and he bit his haughty lip at the thought that he could devise no further humiliation than to make them kneel and lick the sand on which he stood.

They held the mistletoe which grew on the oak sacred, and on the sixth day of the moon came in solemn procession to the tree on which it grew, and offered up sacrifice, and prepared a feast beneath its hallowed branches, adorning themselves with its leaves, as if they could never sufficiently reverence the tree on which the mistletoe grew, although they named themselves druids after the oak.

White bulls were dragged into the ceremony; their stiff necks bowed, and their broad foreheads bound to the stem of the tree, while their loud bellowings came in like a wild chorus to the rude anthem which was chaunted on the occasion: these were slaughtered, and the morning sacrifice went streaming up among the green branches.

The chief druid ascended the oak, treading haughtily upon the bended backs and broad shoulders of the blinded slaves, who struggled to become stepping-stones beneath his feet, and eagerly bowed their necks that he might trample upon them, while he gathered his white garment in his hand, and drew it aside, lest it should become sullied by touching their homely apparel.

Below him stood his brother idolators, their spotless garments outspread ready to catch the falling sprigs of the mistletoe as they dropped beneath the stroke of the golden pruning-knife. Doubtless the solemn mockery ended by the assembled multitude carrying home with them a leaf or a berry each, of the all-healing plant, as it was called, while the druids lingered behind to consume the fatted sacrifice, and forge new fetters to bind down their ignorant followers to their heathenish creed.

Still it is on record that they taught their disciples many things concerning the stars and their motion; that they pretended to some knowledge of distant countries, and the nature of the gods they worshipped. Gildas, one of the earliest of our British historians, seeming to write from what he saw, tells us that their idols almost surpassed in number those of Egypt, and that monuments were then to be seen (in his day) of

> "hideous images, whose frigid, ever-lowering, and depraved countenances still frown upon us both within and outside the walls of deserted cities. We shall not recite the names that once were heard on our mountains, that were repeated at our fountains, that were echoed on our hills, and were pronounced over our rivers, because the honours due to the Divinity alone were paid to them by a blinded people."

That their religion was but a system of long-practised imposture admits not of a doubt; and as we have proof that they possessed considerable knowledge for that period, it is evident that they had recourse to these devices to delude and keep in subjection their fellow-men, thereby obtaining a power which enabled them to live in comparative idleness and luxury. Such were the ancient Egyptian priests; and such, with but few exceptions, were all who, for many centuries, held mighty nations in thrall by the mystic powers with which they cunningly clothed idolatry. True, there might be amongst their

number a few blinded fanatics, who were victims to the very deceit which they practised upon others, whose faculties fell prostrate before the imaginary idols of their own creation, and who bowed down and worshipped the workmanship of their own hands.

All the facts we are in possession of show that they contributed nothing to the support of the community; they took no share in war, though they claimed their portion of the plunder obtained from it; they were amenable to no tribunal but their own, but only sat apart in their gloomy groves, weaving their dangerous webs in darker folds over the eyes of their blinded worshippers. We see  dimly through the shadows of those ancient forests where the druids dwelt; but amongst the forms that move there we catch glimpses of women sharing in their heathen rites; it may be of young and beautiful forms, who had the choice offered them, whether they would become sacrifices in the fires which so often blazed before their grim idols, or share in the solemn mockeries which those darksome groves enshrouded – those secrets which but to whisper abroad would have been death.

The day of reckoning at last came – as it is ever sure to come – and heavy was the vengeance which alighted upon those bearded druids; instead of such living and moving evils, the mute marble of the less offensive gods which the Romans worshipped usurped the places where their blood-stained sacrifices were held.

Jupiter frowned coldly down in stone, but he injured not. Mars held his pointed spear aloft, but the dreaded blow never descended.

They saw the form of man worshipped, and though far off, it was still a nearer approach to the true Divinity than the wicker idol surrounded with flames, and filled with the writhing and shrieking victims who expired in the midst of indescribable agonies.

Hope sat there mute and sorrowful, with her head bowed, and her finger upon her lip, listening for the sound of those wings which she knew would bring Love and Mercy to her aid. She turned not her head to gaze upon those heathenish priests as they were dragged forward to deepen the inhuman stain which sunk deep into the dyed granite of the altar, for she knew that the atmosphere their breath had so long poisoned must be purified before the Divinity could approach; for that bright star which was to illume the world had not yet arisen in the east.

The civilized heathen was already preparing the way in the wilderness, and sweeping down the ruder barbarism before him. There were Roman galleys before, and the sound of the gospel-trumpet behind; and those old oaks jarred again to their very roots, and the huge circus of Stonehenge shook to its broad centre; for the white cliffs that looked out over the sea were soon to echo back a strange language, for Roman cohorts, guided by Julius Cæsar, were riding upon the waves.

4 THE LANDING OF JULIUS CÆSAR

> The cliffs themselves are bulwarks strong: the shelves
> And flats refuse great ships: the coast so open
> That every stormy blast may rend their cables,
> Put them from anchor: suffering double war –
> Their men pitched battle – their ships stormy fight;
> For charges 'tis no season to dispute,
> Spend something, or lose all.
>
> – *The True Trojans*, 1633

Few generals could put in a better plea for invading a country than that advanced by Julius Cæsar, for long before he landed in this island, he had had to contend with a covert enemy in the Britons, who frequently threw bodies of armed men upon the opposite coasts, and by thus strengthening the enemy's ranks, protracted the war he had so long waged with the Gauls.

To chastise the hardy islanders, overawe and take possession of their country, were but common events to the Roman generals, and Cæsar no doubt calculated that to conquer, he had only to show his well-disciplined troops. He was also well aware that the language and religion of the Britons and Gauls were almost the same, and that the island on which his eye was fixed was the great centre and stronghold of the druids; and, not ignorant of the power of these heathen priests, whose mysterious rites banded nation with nation, he doubtless thought that if he could but once overthrow their altars, he could the more easily march over the ruins to more extended conquests.

He had almost the plea of self-defence for setting out to invade England as he did, and such, in reality, is the reason he assigns; and not to possess the old leaven of ambition to strengthen his purpose, was to lack that which, in a Roman general, swelled into the glory of fame.

Renown was the pearl Julius Cæsar came in quest of; he was not a general to lead his legions back to the imperial city, when, after having humbled the pride of the Gauls, he still saw from the opposite coast the island of the presumptuous Britons – barbarians, who had dared to hurl their pointed javelins in the very face of the Roman eagle; – not a man to return home, when, by stretching his arm over that narrow sea, he could gather such laurels as had never yet decked a Roman brow.

The rumour of his intended invasion had already reached the Britons, who, well aware of the victories he had won in the opposite continent, and probably somewhat shaken by the terror which was attached to the name of the Roman conqueror, lost no time in sending over ambassadors with an offer of submission, and hostages.

But although Cæsar received the messengers kindly, and sent back with them Comius, a Gaul, in whose talent and integrity he had the greatest confidence, still his attention was not to be diverted from the object he had in view; and much as he commended their pacific promises, he but waited the return of the galley he had sent out to reconnoitre, before he embarked.

Nor had he to wait long, for on the fifth day after his departure, Volusenus returned from his expedition, with the meagre information he had been able to glean about the coast without landing; though, such as it was, it induced Cæsar to set sail at once, and, with twelve thousand men and eighty transports, he started from the sea coast which stretches between Calais and Boulogne, and steered for the pale-faced cliffs of Albion.

It was in a morning early in autumn, and before the Britons had gathered in their corn-harvest, when the Roman general first

reached the British shore; nor can we, from the force which accompanied him, suppose that he was at all surprised to see the white cliffs of Dover covered with armed men ready to oppose his landing.

But he was too wary a commander to attempt this in so unfavourable a spot, and in the face of such a force, and therefore resolved to lie by, until past the hour of noon, and await the arrival of the remainder of his fleet; for beside the force which we have already enumerated, there were eighteen transports in which his cavalry were embarked, but these were not destined to take a share in his first victory; so finding both wind and tide in his favour, he, without their aid, sailed six or seven miles further down the coast, until he reached the low and open shore which stretches between Walmer Castle and Sandwich.

This manœuvre, however, was not lost upon the Britons, for as he measured his way over the sea, so they kept pace with him upon the land, and when he reached the spot which was so soon to be the scene of slaughter, he found the British army drawn up ready

to receive him, with their cavalry and war-chariots placed in the order of battle, while many a half-naked and hardy soldier stood knee-deep amongst the breakers, which beat upon the beach, with pointed javelin, and heavy club, and rough-hewn war-hatchet, eager to oppose his landing.

The proud Roman himself confesses that they presented a bold front, and made a brave defence. Superior military skill, and long-practised discipline, together with the formidable war-engines which he brought over in his galleys, and from which showers of missiles were projected that spread death and consternation around, were all too much for the Britons, few of whom, except such as had fought in the ranks of the Gauls on the opposite shore, had ever before looked upon such terrible instruments of destruction; and under cover of these, after a short contest, the Roman general managed to disembark two of his legions.

If not for this mode of warfare, and those dreadful engines opening so suddenly upon them, Cæsar would probably never have been able to land his forces; for we may readily imagine that, unaccustomed as they were to such a mode of attack, the consternation that it spread could scarcely be exceeded by a first-class line-of-battle ship pouring in a broadside amongst the startled savages of the South Sea Islands, whose shores had never before echoed back the thunder of a cannon.

Although Cæsar himself states that for a time the Roman soldiers were reluctant to leave their ships, owing to the extent of water which flowed between them and the shore, still there is but little doubt that the fearless front presented by the Britons, as they stood knee-deep among the waves, in spite of the missiles which were sent forth in showers from the Roman galleys, somewhat appalled their highly disciplined invaders.

Cæsar has left it on record that his soldiers hesitated to land, until one of his standard-bearers, belonging to the tenth legion, sprang from the side of the galley into the sea, and waving the ensign over his head, exclaimed, "Follow me, my fellow-soldiers! unless you will give up your eagle to the enemy. I, at least, will do my duty to the republic and to our general!" It was then, roused by the example of the courageous standard-bearer, that the Roman soldiers quitted their ships, and the combatants met hand to hand.

Although upon that ancient battle-ground have the winds and waves for nearly two thousand years beaten, and scarcely a name is left of those who fought, and fell, and dyed the stormy sea-beach with their blood; still, as we gaze down the dim vista of years, the mind's eye again catches glimpses of the unknown combatants – of the warm autumn sunshine falling upon those white and distant cliffs – of the high-decked Roman galleys rising above the ever-moving waves, and we seem to hear the deep voice of the Roman general rising beyond the murmur of the ocean; we see the gilded eagle rocking and swaying over the contending ranks, as they are driven forward or repulsed, just as the tide of battle ebbs and flows; and ever upon the beaten beach where the waves come and go, they wash over some mangled and prostrate form, throwing up here a helmet and there a shield, while figures of the mailed Roman, and the half-naked Briton, lie dead and bleeding side by side, their deep sleep unbroken by the shout, and tramp, and tumult of war. The javelin with its leather thong lies useless beside the bare brawny arm that could hurl it to within an inch of its mark, then recover it again without stepping from out the ranged rank; the dreaded spear lies broken, and the sharp head trodden deep into the sand by a Roman footstep.

Higher up the beach, we hear the thunder of the scythe-wheeled war-chariots of the Britons, and catch glimpses of the glittering and outstretched blades, as they sparkle along in their swift career like a silvery meteor, and all we can trace of their course is the zig-zag pathway streaked with blood. Faint, and afar off, we hear the voices of the bearded druids hymning their war-chaunt, somewhere beyond the tall summits of the bald-faced cliffs.

Anon, the roar of battle becomes more indistinct – slowly and reluctantly the Britons retreat, the Roman soldiers pursue them not, but fall back again upon their galleys, and we hear only a few groans, and the lapping of the waves upon the sea-shore.

And such might have been a brief summary of that combat, interspersed here and there with the daring deeds of warriors whose names will never be known; and then the eye of the imagination closes upon the scene, and all again is enveloped in the deep darkness of nearly two thousand years.

As the Roman cavalry had not yet arrived, Cæsar was prevented from following up the advantage he had gained over the Britons, and marching to where they were encamped, a little way within the island.

The natives, however, doubtless to gain time, and better prepare themselves for a second attack, sent messengers to the Roman general, who were deputed to offer hostages as a guarantee of their submission to the Roman arms. They also liberated Comius, whom he had sent over with offers of alliance; and after a sharp rebuke, in which the Roman invader no doubt attempted to show how wrong it was on their part to attempt to oppose his landing and seizing upon their island, he forgave them, on condition that they would send him a given number of hostages, and allow him, without interference, to act as he chose for the future.

Such, in spirit, were the terms on which the haughty conqueror dismissed the British chiefs, who probably returned with the determination of breaking them whenever an opportunity presented itself. A few hostages were, however, delivered, and several of the British leaders presented themselves before Cæsar, perhaps as covert spies, although they came with avowed offers of allegiance, smarting as they were under their recent defeat.

The Roman general was not destined to accomplish his conquest without meeting with some disasters. The vessels which

contained his cavalry, and were unable to accompany the first portion of his fleet, were again doomed to be driven back by a tempest upon the coast of Gaul, even after they had approached so near the British shore as to be within view of Cæsar's encampment.

The fatal night that saw his cavalry dashed back upon the opposite coast also witnessed the destruction of several of his galleys, which were drawn up on the beach behind his encampment; while those that were lying at anchor in the distant roadstead were either wrecked or cast upon the shore, and so battered by the winds and waves as to be wholly unfit for sea-service; for a high tide seemed to have rushed over his galleys; and this, together with the storm, scarcely left him in the possession of a vessel in which he could put out to sea with his troops.

Without either provisions to feed his soldiers, or materials to repair his shattered ships, and his whole camp deeply dispirited by these unforeseen calamities, the Roman general found himself, at the close of autumn, on a stormy and unfriendly coast, and in possession of but little more of the island than the barren beach on which he had won his hitherto useless victory.

The Britons were not long before they discovered the full extent of these disasters; frequent visits to the Roman encampment had also made them better acquainted with the number of the troops; and as they had already measured their strength against the Roman arms, and the Roman weapons had doubtless lost much of their former terror in their eyes, they began to make preparations for sweeping off the whole force of the invading army, for they clearly saw that it was without either provisions, cavalry, or ships; and though they commenced their work cautiously, they made sure of obtaining an easy victory, and such as they thought would intimidate the hearts of all future invaders.

Cæsar was too wary a general not to see through their designs, for he perceived that the visits of the chiefs to his encampment were less frequent than formerly; that they were also slow in sending in the hostages they had promised to give up; so, Roman-like, he determined to arm himself against the worst.

He ordered some of his troops to repair such ships as were sea-worthy, out of the wreck of those which were useless; these, when ready, he sent over to Gaul for stores; others of his soldiers he sent out to scour the country in search of provisions, and to gather in whatever corn they could find, which must have been very trifling, as he states that, except in one field, all beside in the neighbourhood had been harvested. In this field, which stood at a short distance from one of those old primeval forests which everywhere abounded in the island, one of his legions were busily engaged gathering in corn, when they were suddenly attacked by the armed islanders, who rushed out of their hiding-places from the neighbouring thicket. Fortunately for the Roman soldiers, this chanced to be no great distance from their encampment; and as the ever-watchful eye of Cæsar was open while he stood looking out from his strong fortifications, he saw a huge cloud of dust rising in the air in the direction of the distant corn-field, and sallying out of the encampment, at the head of two of his cohorts, he bade the remainder of the legion follow him with the utmost speed, and rushed off to the rescue of his soldiers.

A few more minutes and he would have arrived too late to save any of them, for he found his legion, which had already suffered considerable loss, hemmed in on every side by the cavalry and war-chariots of the Britons; and he had no sooner succeeded in withdrawing his engaged forces from the corn-field, than he hurried back to his strong entrenchments, the brave islanders having compelled him to make a hasty retreat.

Several days of heavy rain followed, during which the Roman general confined his soldiers to the camp. But the hardy Britons were not to be deterred by the elements from following up the slight advantage which they had gained; so mustering a strong force of both horse and foot, they drew up and surrounded the Roman entrenchments.

Cæsar was too brave to sit quietly and be trapped in his own stronghold by an army of barbarians; so watching a favourable moment, he marshalled forth his mailed legions, which were by this time strengthened by a small body of cavalry that had returned with Comius from Gaul; and with these he fell upon the Britons and dispersed them with great slaughter, also pursuing them into the country, and setting fire to many of their huts, before he again returned to his encampment.

The Britons, as before, sued for peace, which Cæsar readily granted, as he was anxious to return to Gaul with his leaky ships and wearied troops; nor did he wait to receive the offered hostages, but with the first fair wind set sail, having gained little more than hard blows by this, his first invasion.

The warm spring days which brought back the swallow from over the sea saw the Roman galleys again riding on the sunny waves that broke upon our rock-girt coast. From the surrounding heights and smooth slopes which dipped gently down into the sea, the assembled Britons beheld eight hundred vessels of various sizes hastening shoreward from the opening ocean.

Amid waving crests and glittering coats of mail, and Roman eagles blazing like gold in the distance, and long javelins whose points shone like silver in the sunlight, as they rose high above the decks of the galleys, they came rolling along like a moving forest of spears, swayed aside for a moment as some restive war-steed, impatient to plant his sharp hoof upon the earth, jerked his haughty neck, and shook out his long dark mane upon the refreshing breeze, while his shrill neigh came ringing upon the beach above the hoarse murmur of the breakers, which rolled at the feet of the terrified Britons.

On those decks were assembled more than thirty thousand Roman soldiers, headed again by Julius Cæsar, and now strengthened by two thousand cavalry.

It is said that the excuse offered by the Roman general for this second invasion was that hostages had not been sent in according to treaty, though the truth beyond doubt is that his ambition was dissatisfied with the hasty retreat he had been compelled to make. His pride had been mortified at the bold front the islanders had presented, for he must have felt, in his hurried departure to Gaul, that he bore back but little to entitle him to the much-coveted name of Conqueror, a name which his wars with the Britons never won him, for even Tacitus deigned to honour him with little more than the title of Discoverer, after all his exploits in our island had terminated.

Unlike his former reception, he this time landed without having to strike a blow, for the sight of such an armed host struck terror into the hearts of the natives, and they fled in the direction of the Stour, or near to that neighbourhood where Canterbury now stands.

A proof of how earnestly Cæsar commenced his second campaign in the island, and how resolved he was to bring the war to a speedy end, is found in his setting out at midnight to pursue the Britons, scarcely leaving a sixth part of his army behind to protect his shipping and encampment.

Perchance, the haughty Roman had boasted how soon he would bring over a few of the barbaric chiefs for his friends, and would add to their stock of foreign curiosities a few dozen war-chariots, and he had laughed amongst his officers at the joke of their being picked up by some island warrior, and carried off in his scythe-armed car by a couple of swift-footed steeds. He frequently wrote to Rome, and perhaps occasionally boasted in his epistles, about the speedy work he would make of the conquest of Britain.

Be this as it may, there is proof in the strength of the force which landed this time that he had already begun to appreciate the brave blood that flowed through those ancient British veins.

In the still depth of midnight did the measured tramp of Roman infantry ring upon the silence, as they strode inland towards the heart of Kent, and beside those old forests and reedy morasses was the heavy tread of Cæsar's cavalry heard; the rattle of their mail, and the jingling of their harness, broken by the short answers of the scouts as they rode hastily in and out, announcing a clear course, or with low obeisance receiving the commands of the general.

We may picture some poor peasant startled from his sleep by that armed throng, dragged out of his wattled hut by the side of the wild forest, and rudely handled by the Roman soldiers, because he either refused to tell, or was ignorant of the position his countrymen had taken up. We may picture the herdsman hurrying his flocks into the forest fastnesses as he heard that solemn and distant tramp coming like subdued thunder upon the night breeze, so unlike the wild shoutings and mingled rolling of his own war-chariots, amid which the voices of women and children were ever mingled; so solemn, deep, and orderly would march along those well-disciplined Roman troops, contrasted with the irregular movements of the Britons.

Cæsar reached the reedy margin of a river in the cold grey dawn of a spring morning; and as the misty vapour cleared up from the face of the water, he beheld the hardy islanders drawn up on the rising ground beyond the opposite bank, ready to dispute the passage if he ventured across.

The charge was sounded, and at the first blast of the Roman trumpets, the cavalry dashed into the river, and the well-tempered steel blades of the invaders soon began to hew a path through the opposing ranks, for almost at the first stroke the swords of the Britons, which were made of tin and copper, bent, and became useless, while those wielded by their assailants were double-edged, and left a gash every time they descended. The horses broke through the British infantry as if they had been but a reed fence; and as their cavalry was the heaviest, they met in full career the rush of the island war-chariots, plunged their long javelins into the chests of the horses, and received the shock of the British cavalry on the points of their highly-tempered and strong-shafted spears.

The whole affray seemed more like a skirmish than a regular engagement, as if the war-chariots and cavalry of the Britons were only employed to check the advance of the Roman columns, while the remainder of their force retreated to a strong fortification, which stood at some distance in the woods, and which was barricaded by felled trees, fastened together and piled one above another. Thither the remainder of the army also fled, leaving the Romans to follow after they had regained the order of march, and sent back to their camp those who were wounded in the skirmish on the river bank. These marches through wild, uncultivated forests were very harassing to the heavily-armed Roman legions,

who made but slow progress compared to the light-footed troops of the Britons, for they were inured to this woodland warfare, and as familiar with the forest passes as the antlered deer.

Pursuit was again the order of the day; the stronghold in the forest was taken by the Romans, and amongst the legions which distinguished themselves in the contest was the one which, but for the timely arrival of Cæsar, would probably have left their bones to whiten in the harvest-field from which they had had so narrow an escape in the preceding autumn.

Another evening darkened over the forest, under cover of which the Britons again retreated further inland, without being pursued; for the Roman general seemed to have a dread of those gloomy old woods through which the paths, even in the open noon-day, were rugged, uncertain, and difficult, and were as likely to lead towards some bog, lake, or dangerous morass, as to any of the British fortifications. The Roman soldiers were therefore employed in throwing up intrenchments, and strengthening their position in case of a surprise.

It came, but not until morning, and instead of the Britons, was brought by a party of Roman horsemen from the camp; the galleys were again driven upon the shore by the waves, and many of them wrecked; the angry ocean had once more risen up against the fortunes of Cæsar. These unwelcome tidings arrived just as he had given the order to advance; a few minutes more, and he would have been off in full pursuit after the Britons. The unexplored forest stretched before him; his eagles glittered in the morning sunshine; the trumpets had sounded the march, when the order was given to halt, and more than twenty thousand armed Romans were compelled to return at the bidding of the waves. The mound they had thrown up was deserted; the river, which had but a few hours before been reddened by the blood of many a brave warrior, was repassed without opposition; and both cavalry and infantry now commenced a rapid retreat in the direction of the Roman encampment.

When Cæsar reached the sea-shore, he beheld a sight discouraging enough to blanch even a Roman cheek; many of his finest galleys had become total wrecks; others it seemed almost impossible to repair; the few that were saved he despatched at once to Gaul for assistance. He set every hand that could use a saw, axe, or mallet, immediately to work, and instead of sitting down and bemoaning his ill-fortune, he, like the brave-hearted Roman that he was, began to make up for his loss, and gave orders for building several new ships. Added to this, he had the remainder drawn onto shore, and ran up a barrier to protect them from the ravages of the ocean, thus including a dry-dock within his fortified encampment. All these preparations necessarily consumed some time, during which the islanders remained undisturbed.

*

Returning to the Britons, who had not been idle during this brief interval, we find their army greatly increased, and a renowned prince, named Cassivellaunus, placed as commander at their head – they wisely judging that one who had so distinguished himself in his wars with the neighbouring tribes was best fitted to lead them on, now that they were banded together for mutual protection against the Romans. Nobly did the barbaric chief acquit himself; he waited not to be attacked; but having selected his own battle-ground, charged upon the Roman cavalry at once, with his horsemen and war-chariots.

Although Cæsar did at last gain a slight victory – and, as he himself says, drove the Britons into the woods, and lost several of his soldiers through venturing too far – still it does not appear that he obtained the day, for the Britons already began to find the advantages they obtained through occasional retreats, which enabled them to draw the enemy either nearer to, or into the woods – a stratagem which in this skirmish they availed themselves of; for while the Romans were busy, as was their custom, in protecting their camp for the night, by throwing up ramparts and digging trenches around it, the Britons sallied out from another opening in the wood, and slaughtered the outer guard.

The Roman general ordered two cohorts to advance to the rescue; they were also repulsed, and a tribune was slain; fresh troops were summoned into action, and the Britons betook themselves to their old leafy coverts with but very little loss.

On this occasion, the Roman general was compelled to acknowledge, that his heavy-armed soldiers were no match for an enemy who only retreated one moment to advance with greater force the next, and would, whenever an opportunity presented itself, dismount from their horses, or leap out of their chariots, and renew the battle on foot, and that, too, on the very edge of some dangerous bog, where an armed horseman was sure to founder if he but made a leap beyond the boundary line with which they were so familiar.

Another day, a disastrous one for the Britons, and the battle was renewed, and they, as before, commenced the attack, waiting, however, until the Roman general had sent out a great portion of his cavalry and infantry to forage – a body amounting to more than half his army, no mean acknowledgment of the estimation in which the island force was held, while it required from ten to fifteen thousand men to collect the supplies he needed for one day; a tolerable proof that he had not forgotten the all but fatal skirmish in the corn-field when he first landed.

Emboldened by their success on the previous day, the Britons this time charged up to the solid body of the Roman legions, rushing fearlessly against the wall which their well-disciplined ranks presented – a firm phalanx, the formation that had withstood the shock of the bravest armies in Europe without being broken; an array strengthened every moment by the return of the foragers.

One solid, impenetrable mass now bore down, like a mighty avalanche, upon the congregated Britons; a vast sea of spears, and

shields, and swords, all heaving onward without resistance, Cæsar heralding the way, like the God of the storm, the armed cavalry thundering onward like the foremost wave, until the whole mass struck upon the iron stems of the gnarled oaks which stood at the edge of the forest, then rolled back again into the plain, leaving a line of wounded and dead to mark their destructive course. It was the first open shore on which the full tide of the Roman arms had flowed on the islanders. The waves had many a time before gathered together and broken, but here the full surge of battle swept uninterrupted upon the beach. Although the sun still sets over that great graveyard of the dead, not a monument remains to tell of its whereabouts, or to point out the spot where many a brave soldier took his rest.

Through Kent, and along the valley which stretches at the foot of the Surrey hills, Cæsar pursued the shattered army of the British prince, his march probably extending over that level line of beautiful meadow-land on which the old palace of Eltham still stands, along the wooded neighbourhood of Penge and Sydenham, and out at the foot of the Norwood hills, to where, far beyond, the Thames still glitters like a belt of silver as it goes winding round near Chertsey.

Here the British leader had rallied; on the opposite bank stood his forces, and in the bed of the river he had caused pointed stakes to be planted, to prevent his pursuers from crossing the ford. These were but slight obstacles in the path of Cæsar; he ordered his cavalry to advance, commanded the infantry to follow at their heels, or at their sides, as they best could; and so they passed, some grasping the manes of the war-horses with one hand to steady their steps in the current, while with the other they held the double-edged sword, ready to hew or thrust, the moment they came within arm's length of the enemy.

Cassivellaunus was once more compelled to retreat, though never so far but that he was always in readiness to fall upon any detached cohorts, and with his five thousand war-chariots to hang upon and harass any party of foragers.

Cæsar was at last compelled to send out his legions to protect the horsemen while they gathered in provisions. Even then, the island prince drove and carried off all the cattle and corn which was pastured or garnered in the neighbourhood of the Roman encampment.

The invaders were never safe except when within their own entrenchments; for they had now to deal with an enemy who had grown too wary to trust himself again in the open field, but contented himself by harassing and attacking any detached Roman units which he could waylay. He was well acquainted with all the secret passes and intricate roads, and kept the Roman guards in a continual state of alarm. When it was not safe to attack, the Britons would at times assemble at the

outskirts of the woods, and shaking their javelins, to the foot of which a hollow ball of copper containing lumps of metal or pebbles was affixed, commence such a sudden thundering and shouting as startled the horses, and caused them to run affrighted in every direction; they then seized upon the forage, and before the heavy legions could overtake them, they were off at full speed far away in the forest passes, along paths known only to themselves. Such a system of warfare was new to Cæsar, and as yet he had only gained the ground he was encamped upon. That which contained his army, for the time, was all he could call his own.

But the Britons could not long remain true to themselves; petty jealousies and long-stifled murmurs began at last to find vent. One tribe after another came to the Roman camp; to all he made fair promises, took their corn and their hostages, sowing no doubt the seeds of dissension deeper amongst them at the same time, and getting them also to inform him where the capital of their warlike chief was situated. This secret they were base enough to betray; for many of the petty princes envied the renown which Cassivellaunus had won by his valour.

Even Cæsar's narrative at this turn of events enlists our sympathies on the side of the British general and the handful of brave followers who still remained true to their country's cause. His capital, which is supposed to have stood on the site of St Albans, and which in those days was surrounded by deep woods and broad marshes, was attacked. Many were slain, some prisoners taken, and numbers of cattle driven away; for the forest town of this courageous chief appears to have been nothing more than a cluster of woodland huts surrounded by a ditch, and strengthened by a rampart of mud and trees, a work which the Roman legions would level to the earth in a brief space of time.

Though beaten and forced from his capital, the British prince retreated upon another fortress further into the wood; from this he was also driven. Yet still his great heart buoyed him up; and although defeated, he determined to have another struggle for the liberty of his unworthy country, and despatched messengers into Kent, bidding the Britons to fall at once upon the Roman camp and fleet.

Had the prince himself been present, it is not improbable that this daring deed would have been executed, for he was unequalled in falling upon the enemy, and carrying his point by surprise – but he was not; and although the attack did honour to the valour of the brave men of Kent, it failed. Many were slain, and the Romans returned victorious to their camp. It wanted but the genius who meditated so bold a stroke to have carried it into effect; had he been there, Cæsar's eagles would never more have spread out their golden wings beneath the triumphal arches of haughty Rome.

Fain would we here drop the curtain over the name of this ancient British warrior, and leave him to sleep in the heart of his high-piled barrow undisturbed. Alas, he was compelled to sue to the Roman general for peace, who no doubt offered it to him willingly, conscious that, had he succeeded in his bold attempt upon the camp and fleet, the Roman would have had to kneel for the same grant at the foot of the Briton.

Cæsar demanded hostages, got them, and hurried off to his ships, and without leaving a Roman troop behind, hastened with all his force to the coast of Gaul, and never again did he set foot upon our island shore.

Over the future career of Cassivellaunus the deep midnight of oblivion has settled; the waves of time have washed no further record upon that vast shore which is strewn over with the wrecks of so many mighty deeds; the assembled druids who chaunted his requiem, and the Cymric or Celtic bard who in rude rhymes broke the forest echoes as he recounted his exploits in battle, have all passed away; and but for the pen of his Roman opponent, we should never have known the bravery of that British heart, which, nearly two thousand years ago, beat with hopes and fears like our own.

5 CARACTACUS, BOADICEA, AND AGRICOLA

And many an old man's sigh, and many a widow's,
And many an orphan's water-standing eye –
Men for their sons', wives for their husbands' fate,
And orphans for their parents' timeless death –
Did rue the hour that ever thou wert born.

– *Shakspeare*

For nearly a century after the departure of Cæsar, we have no records of the events which transpired in England; that the inhabitants made some progress in civilization during that period is all we know; for there can be but little doubt that a few of the Roman soldiers remained behind, and settled in the island after the first invasion, and introduced some degree of refinement amongst the tribes with whom they peaceably dwelt.

No attempt, however, was made, during this long interval, to fortify the island against any future invasion; and when the Roman commander Plautius landed, about ninety-seven years after the departure of Cæsar, he met with no resistance until he had led his army some distance into the inland country. After a time a few skirmishes took place – some of the tribes submitted – but nothing like a determined resistance seems to have been offered to the Roman arms, until Plautius had extended his victories beyond the Severn, and compelled the Britons to retreat into the marshes beside the Thames.

Here it was that the Roman commander first learned to estimate aright the valour of the force he had to contend against; for the bogs and swamps which had so often checked the meditated movements of Cæsar proved nearly fatal to the force headed by Plautius, who, after suffering a severe loss, retreated to a secure position beside the Thames.

In this strong encampment that he calmly awaited the arrival of the Emperor Claudius, who, after a time, joined him with a considerable reinforcement – just stayed long enough to look round him – received the submission of a few petty states – and then returned most triumphantly to Rome; for it is questionable whether he ever fought a single battle.

It is at this period that the figure of Caractacus heaves up slowly above the scene; we see him but dimly and indistinctly at first, but, after a time, he towers above all his compeers, as Cassivellaunus did in the days of Cæsar. We see him moving now and then between the divided legions commanded by Vespasian and Plautius, but nothing of importance is done on either side.

The Isle of Wight is for a short time subdued; a small portion of the island south of the Thames is occupied by the invaders; then Plautius is recalled to Rome, and before he well arrives at the imperial city, the whole camp is in disorder; the Roman legions can no longer protect the states that have submitted to them.

Caractacus is up, armed, and in earnest.

Ostorius Scapula next appears, and places himself at the head of the Roman ranks, strikes an unexpected blow in the midst of winter, and gains

some advantage over the Britons. About this time it appears that the Romans first commenced the erection of forts in the island, thus keeping the conquered states within well-guarded lines, and protecting them from the attacks of the unsubdued tribes, taking good care, at the same time, that they did not escape and join their independent countrymen.

His next step was to disarm all the states within these limits; and as some of them had become willing allies, rebellion soon broke out within these circumscribed bounds. Once disarmed, it will readily be imagined how easily they were beaten. Ostorius had now work enough on his hands; the tribes that occupied the present counties of York and Lancashire next arose, attacked the Roman legions, and were defeated.

It was then that the ancient Silures sprang up, the bravest of all the British tribes, the true Cimbrii of early renown. The battle-ground now shifts into Wales, and Caractacus is the commander.

Almost every mountain-pass and ford were familiar to him; his renown already rang through the island; wherever the Roman eagle had bowed its haughty neck, he had been present; the Roman general knew with whom he had to deal, and moved forward with all his available force. Around the standard of Caractacus had rallied every tribe from the surrounding country who refused to bow their necks to the invaders.

Tacitus says that he chose his ground with great skill, in the centre of steep and difficult hills, raising ramparts of massive stones, where the ascent was possible. Between his army and the road by which the Romans must approach, there flowed a river which it was difficult to ford.

As the enemy drew near, he exhorted his soldiers to remember how their forefathers had driven Cæsar from Britain, spoke to them of freedom, their homes, their wives and children, in a style which the Roman historians would have pronounced eloquent, had the address flowed from the mouth of one of their own generals.

But again the Britons were conquered, though they fought bravely – their naked bosoms and helmetless heads were sure marks for well-tempered Roman blades, while their own copper swords bent back at the first thrust they made at their mail-clad enemies. Caractacus was not slain. He escaped, only to be given up in chains to the Romans by his treacherous stepmother, Cartismanda, after having for nine years waged war against the invaders of Britain.

The British leader, along with his wife and children, was taken as a prisoner to Rome; his fame had flown before him, and the Romans, who ever respected valour, crowded round to look at the renowned island chief. He alone, of all the British captives, shrunk not when brought before the Roman emperor, Claudius. There was a noble bearing about the man: that eye which had never quailed before the keen edge of the uplifted blade in battle – that heart which had never sunk, though it was the last to retreat from the hard fought field, buoyed him up in the presence of his enemy, and the Roman emperor ordered his chains to be struck off, an act which did honour to the successor of Cæsar. Caractacus would have done the same, had Claudius obtained the same renown, and so stood a captive before him.

Whether the brave barbarian died in some contest with a gladiator in the arena of Rome, butchered as part of a holiday event, in a later day, before Nero, or returned to his country, or joined the legions of his conquerors, and fell fighting in some foreign land, we know not – we only see his chains struck off before the Emperor Claudius, and then he vanishes forever from the pages of history.

Even this undoubted victory was of but little advantage to the Roman arms.

The Silures proved themselves worthy descendants of the ancient Cymry, the terror of whose name, as we have before shown, had in former times carried consternation to the very gates of Rome. They broke up the enemy's camp, fell upon their lines and forts, drove the Roman legions back to their old entrenchments, and, but for the timely arrival of a party of foragers, would have cut up every soldier within the Roman encampment in Wales.

Nor could Ostorius, when he brought up all his legions to battle, conquer them again. One skirmish was but the forerunner of another; the Britons but retreated today, to advance with stronger force on the morrow; until at last, harassed and vexed, ever fighting but obtaining no advantage, the commander, who had conquered Caractacus, fortified himself within his camp, and died. He was the bravest general that the Britons had ever looked upon since the days of Cæsar. Pass we by Frontinus, Didius, and Veranius; there are other shadows to pass over this dimly lit stage of our history, who will do strange deeds, and then depart.

Wearied and harassed by such a succession of invasions, the chiefs of the druids, with many of the Britons who refused to submit to the Roman yoke, retired to the island of Anglesey, that they might, amid its shadowy groves and deep passes, follow their religious rites without molestation, and sleep securely without being aroused by the din of arms which was ever awakening the echoes that dwelt amongst gloomy Albion's white cliffs.

To this island, guarded more by the terrors of superstition than any substantial array of arms, the Roman commander, Paulinus Suetonius, determined to cross; and to accomplish his purpose, he built a number of flat-bottomed boats in which he placed his troops.

As the invading force neared the opposite shore, they were struck with terror by the strange scene which rose before them, and many a Roman heart that had never before quailed in the stormy front of battle stood appalled before the dreaded array which had there congregated. It seemed as if they had reached the shores of the fabulous Hades of their ancient poets; for there women were seen rushing in every direction in dresses on which were woven the forms of dismal objects; and while their long dishevelled hair streamed out in the sea breeze, they brandished their flaming torches aloft as they rushed to and fro, their eyes glaring wildly out of the dense smoke, as it blew back again in their angry faces, while they looked out, as fierce as the furies, and as terrible as hell.

Behind them were the grim druids collected, with hands and eyes uplifted, as they invoked the curses of the gods upon the heads of the Roman legions; before them the huge fires which were already kindled blazed and crackled and shot out their consuming tongues of flame, as if they were hungry for their prey, while the druids pointed to the invading force, and bade their warriors hasten and bring their victims to the sacrifice.

The Roman soldiers seemed paralysed; they stood almost motionless, as if they had not the power to strike a blow. They fell back affrighted before the lighted torches of the women, and the curses of the druids, which struck more terror into their souls than if the thunder of a thousand war chariots had borne down upon them, in all their headlong array.

Aroused at last by the voice of their leader, who bade them to despise a force of frantic women and praying priests, they rushed boldly on, even to the very foot of the dreaded fires; and many a bearded druid was that day driven before the points of the Roman spears into the devouring flames which  they had kindled for the destruction of their invaders.

Dreadful was the carnage that ensued; even the sacred groves were fired or cut down; if the Britons escaped the flames, it was but to rush back again upon the points of the Roman swords – the sun sunk upon a scene of desolation and death – a landscape blackened with ashes – fires that had been extinguished by blood, whose grey embers faded and died out, as the last sobs of the expiring victims subsided into the eternal silence of death.

*

The spirit of British vengeance, though asleep, was not yet dead. At the rumour of these dreadful deeds it sprang up, awake and armed, on the opposite shore; as if the blow which struck down their sacred groves and overthrew their ancient altars had sent a shock across the straits of Menai, which had been felt throughout the whole length and breadth of the land; as if at the fall of the sacred groves of Mona the spirits of the departed dead had rushed across, while the voices of the murdered druids filled all the air with their wailing cries of

lamentation, until even women sprang up demanding vengeance, and Boadicea leaped into her war chariot, as if to rebuke the British warriors by her presence, and to show them that the soul of a woman, loathing their abject slavery, was ready to lead them on to either liberty or death, and to place her fair form in the dangerous front of battle – for her white shoulders had not escaped the mark of the Roman scourge.

Her daughters had been violated before her eyes, her subjects driven from their homes, the whole territory of the Iceni over which she reigned as queen groaned again beneath the weight of cruelty, and oppression, and wrong. Her subjects were made slaves; her relations were dragged into captivity by the haughty conquerors; her priests slaughtered; her altars overthrown, and another creed thrust into the throats of those over whom she ruled, at the points of the Roman swords. Her sufferings, her birth, the death of her husband king Prasutagus, her towering spirit, her bold demeanour, and the energy of her address, struck like an electric shock throughout all the surrounding tribes, and many a state which had bowed in abject submission beneath the haughty feet of the conquerors, now sprang up, and as if endowed with a new life, rushed onward to the great mustering ground of battle, like clouds hastening up to join the dark mass which gathers about the dreaded thunderstorm, before the deafening explosion bursts forth.

On the Roman colony of Camaladonum did this terrible tempest first break, scattering before it a whole Roman legion, and scarcely leaving one alive behind to tell the tale. The voices of pity

and mercy were unheard amid that dire and revengeful din; no quarter was given, no prisoners were made; blinded with revenge, stung to madness by the remembrance of their grievous wrongs, the assailants rushed forward, sparing neither age nor sex; destruction seemed to have set all her dreadful instruments at once to work, and in a few days upwards of 70,000 Romans perished by the gibbet, the fire, and the sword.

Such of the Roman officers as could escape fled to their galleys, and hurried off to Gaul. Even Suetonius, who had hastened back at the first rumour of this dreadful carnage, was compelled to abandon London, already a place of some distinction, in despair, and hurry off with his legions into the open provinces.

As he retreated, the Britons entered; and out of the vast multitude which a few hours before those walls had inclosed, scarcely a soul remained alive. The Roman soldiers rushed into their temples to avoid the assailants; the figure of the goddess of Victory which they worshipped fell to the ground; the females ran wailing and shrieking into the streets, into the council chambers, into the theatres, with their children in their arms. In the red sunsets of the evening sky their heated imagination traced moving and blood-coloured phantoms, colonies in ruins, and overthrown temples, whose pillars were stained with human gore, and in the ridges which the receding tide left upon the shore, their fancies conjured up the carcases of the dead.

Before the desolating forces of the stern Boadicea ran Fear and Terror, with trembling steps and pale looks; by her side grim Destruction, and blood-dyed Carnage stalked, while behind marched Death, taking no note of Sorrow, and Grief, and Silence, whom he left together to mourn amid the solitude of those unpeopled ruins.

Meantime, Suetonius, having strengthened his army to a force which now amounted to upwards of 10,000 men, chose the most favourable position for his troops, where he awaited the arrival of the Britons to commence the battle. Nor had he to wait long; for, flushed with victory, and reeking fresh from the carnage, the assailants came up, with Boadicea, thundering in her war chariot, at their head, and soon drew together in the order of battle. The Romans wanted revenge.

With her long yellow hair unbound, and falling in clusters far below the golden chain which encircled her waist, her dark eyes

QUEEN BOADICEA LEADING THE BRITONS AGAINST THE ROMANS.

flashing vengeance as she glanced angrily aside to where the Roman legions were drawn up in the distance, an impenetrable mass, looking in their coats of mail like a wall of steel, bristling with swords and spears.

With the curved crimson of her cruel lip haughtily upturned, Boadicea rose tall and queen-like from the war-chariot in which her weeping daughters were seated, and turning to the assembled tribes who hemmed her round with a forest of tall spears, she raised her hand to command silence. When the busy murmur of subdued applause which acknowledged her bravery had died away, she bade them remember the wrongs they had to revenge, the weight of oppression which had so long bowed their necks to the dust; the sword, and fire, and famine which had desolated their fair land; their sons and daughters carried off and doomed to all the miseries of slavery; their priests ruthlessly butchered at the foot of the altar; their ancient groves hewn to the ground by sacrilegious hands and consumed by fire.

She pointed to her daughters whom the invaders had violated, and raising her white and rounded arm, showed the marks which the scourge of the ruffianly Catus had left behind; then brandishing her spear aloft, she shook the loosened reins over her restive steeds, and was soon lost in the thickest of the battle.

But the lapse of a century, and the many battles in which they had fought, had not yet enabled the Britons to stand firm before the shock of the Roman legions. They were defeated with tremendous slaughter; and the queen, who had so nobly revenged her country's wrongs, only escaped the carnage to perish by her own hand.

Even down the dim vista of time we can yet perceive her; the flower of her army lying around her dead; the remnant routed and pursued by the merciless Romans, while she, heartbroken, hopeless and alone, sacrifices her own life; and though but a heathen, performs a deed which in that barbarous age would have ennobled her had she been born in the country of her civilized invaders, who would proudly have erected a statue to her memory in that city whose haughty emperors proclaimed themselves the conquerors of the world. Little did the vanquishers dream that a woman would spring up and emulate the deeds of their most renowned warriors, and that the fair barbarian would in after ages leave behind her a more than Roman name.

But neither the destruction of the druids, nor the death of Boadicea, nor the destruction of her immense army, enabled the Romans to extend their possessions with safety in the island. They were ever, as in the days of Cæsar, on the defensive; no colony, unless a legion of soldiers were encamped in the immediate neighbourhood, was safe; and even after defeating the queen of the Iceni, and receiving a great force of both infantry and cavalry, Suetonius left the island unconquered, the war unfinished, and returned to Rome.

It is a pleasure to turn from these scenes of slaughter to find that the next Roman general of note who came over to govern Britain subdued more tribes by the arts of peace, and by kindness, than all his predecessors had done by the force of arms. Such is the power of genius that we seem again to be in the company of one we have long known; for Agricola was the father-in-law of Tacitus, the eloquent historian, and there is but little doubt that the record of the few facts we are in possession of connected with this period were dictated by the general himself to his highly gifted son-in-law.

We can almost imagine the grey-headed veteran and the author seated together in some Roman villa discoursing about these "deeds of other days." He had served under Suetonius, was present at that dreadful massacre in the island of Anglesey, where men, women, and children were so mercilessly butchered – he had with his own eyes looked upon Boadicea.

What would we not now give to know all that he had seen? To write this portion of our history with his eyes – to go on from page to page recording what he witnessed from day to day – to have him seated by our hearth now as he no doubt many a time sat beside Tacitus. What word-pictures would we then paint – what wild scenes would we portray!

It was Agricola who first taught the ancient Britons to erect better houses, to build walled cities instead of huts; who bestowed praise upon their improvements, instructed them in the Roman language, and persuaded them to adopt a more civilized costume; to erect baths and temples; to improve their agriculture; and thus by degrees he so led them on, from step to step. From being a race of rude barbarians, they began to assume the aspect of a more civilized nation.

Still he had to contend with old and stubborn tribes who believed that it was a disgrace to adopt any other manners than those of their rude forefathers – the same difficulties beset the path of the Norman on a later day – and the same obstacles are met with in Ireland today: pride, indolence, ignorance, and a host of other evils have first to be uprooted before the better seed can be sown.

It would but be wearisome to follow the footsteps of the Roman general through all his campaigns; before him the imperial eagles were borne to the very foot of the Grampian hills; he erected forts for the better protection of the country he had conquered, and the huge rampart which ran from the Frith of Clyde to the Forth was begun under Agricola. He appears to have been the first of the Roman commanders who brought his legions into contact with the Caledonians, or men of the woods, and even there he met with a formidable opponent in the Caledonian chief named Galgacus; and the same struggle for liberty was made there as in England – battles, bloodshed, death, and desolation are about all that history records of these campaigns, if we except what may be called a voyage of discovery; for it appears that the Roman general sailed round the coast of Scotland to the Land's End in Cornwall, and thence to the point from which he had first started – supposed to be Sandwich – so he was the first of the Roman generals who, from personal observation, discovered that Britain was an island. Shortly after completing this voyage Agricola was recalled to Rome.

*

The next period of our history carries us to other conflicts, which took place before those mighty bulwarks that the Roman conquerors built up to keep back the northern invaders, who in their turn overran England with more success than the Romans had done before them. It was then a war between the Romans and the Picts and Scots, instead of, as before, between the Romans and the Britons.

Although they doubtless originally descended from the same Celtic race, yet through the lapse of years, and their having lingered for some time in Ireland and in Gaul, we are entangled in so many doubts, that all we can clearly comprehend is that three different languages were spoken in the island of Britain at this period: namely, Welsh, Irish, and another; but whether the latter was Gothic or Pictish, learned men who have dedicated long years of study to the subject have not yet determined by what name it should be distinguished.

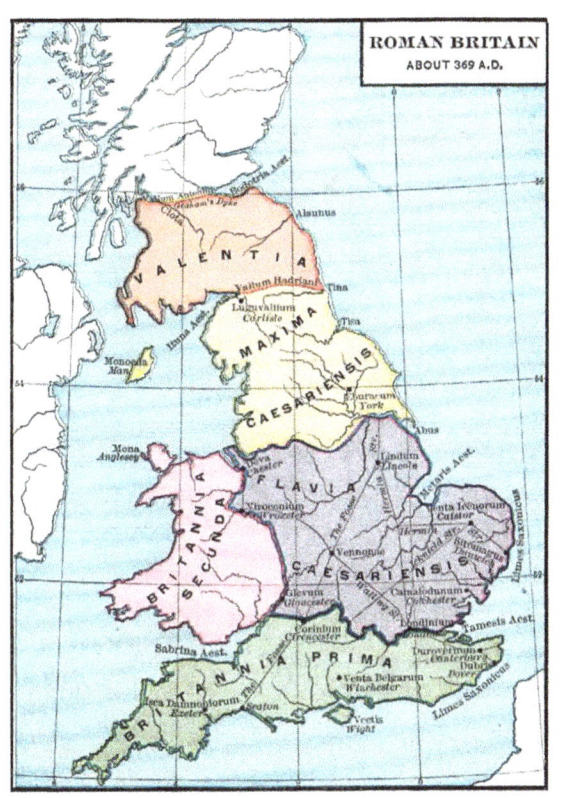

Firth of Forth
Antonine Wall
Begun in AD 142
North
sea
Hadrian's Wall
Begun in AD 122
Irish
sea
NORTH
0 20 40 60 80 100
Kilometres

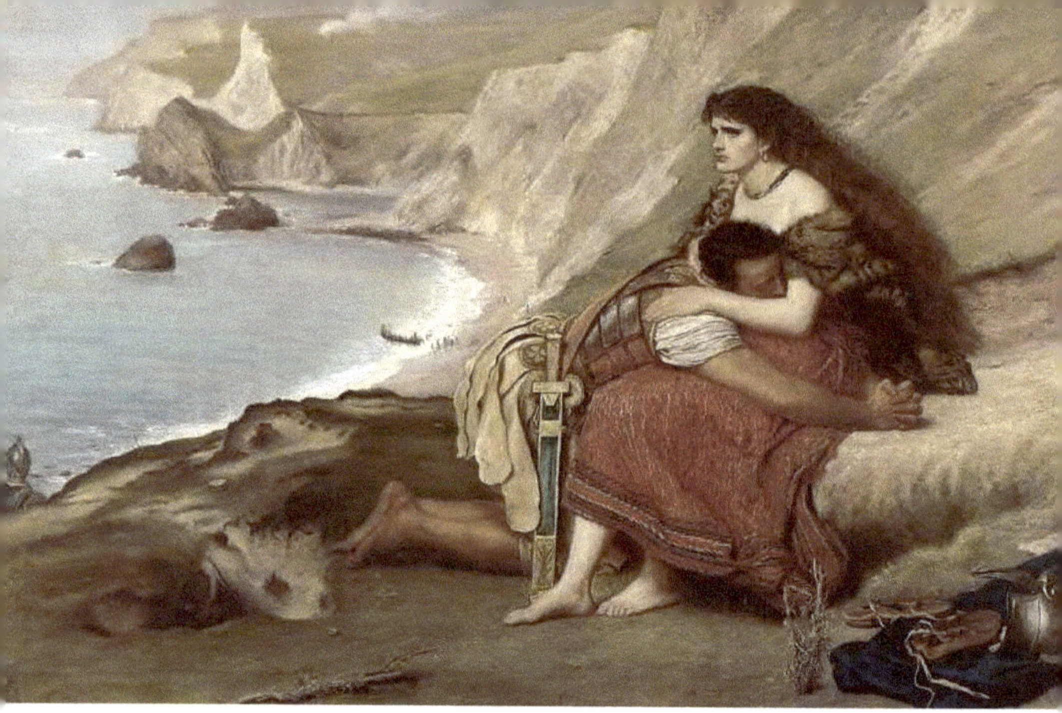

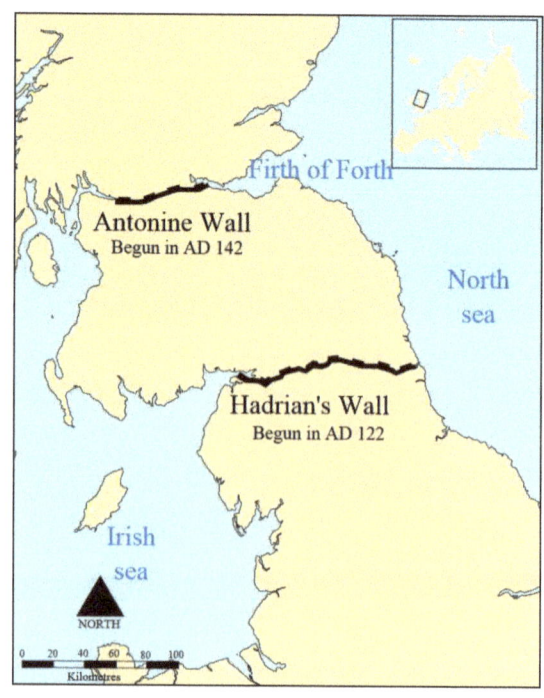

6 THE DEPARTURE OF THE ROMANS

> He looked and saw wide territory spread
> Before him; towns and rural works between,
> Cities of men, with lofty gates and towers,
> Concourse in arms, fierce forces threatening war –
> Assaulting: others, from the wall defend
> With dart and javelin, stones and sulphurous fire:
> On each hand slaughter and gigantic deeds."
>
> – Milton's *Paradise Lost,* Book XI

The fortified line erected by Agricola was soon broken through by the northern tribes, and the Emperor Hadrian erected a much stronger barrier, though considerably within the former; and this extended from the Tyne to the Solway, crossing the whole breadth of that portion of the island.

Urbicus, as if determined that the Romans should not lose an inch of territory which they had once possessed, restored the more northern boundary which Hadrian had abandoned, and once more stretched the Roman frontier between the Friths of Clyde and Forth; they thus possessed two walls, the more northern one, first begun by Agricola, and the southern one, erected by Hadrian.

Forts were built at little more than a mile distant from each other along this line, and a broad rampart ran within the wall, by which troops could readily march from one part to another. This outer barrier was the scene where many a hard contest took place, and in the reign of Commodus it was again broken down, and the country ravaged up to the very foundations of the wall of Adrian. This skirmishing and besieging, building up and breaking down of barriers, lasted for nearly a century, during which period scarcely a single event transpired in Britain of sufficient importance to be recorded, though there is every proof that the Britons were, in the meantime, making rapid strides in civilization; for England rested securely under the guardianship of the Roman arms.

The battles fought at the northern barriers did not disturb the tranquillity of the southern parts of the island. It was not until the commencement of the third century, when old and gouty, and compelled to be borne at the head of his army in a litter, that the Emperor Severus determined to conquer the Caledonians, and boldly sallied out for that purpose beyond the northern frontier. His loss was enormous, and between war with the natives, and the wearisome labour in making roads, felling forests, and draining marshes, which had hitherto been impassable to the Roman troops, 50,000 soldiers were sacrificed.

Nothing daunted, however, the gouty old emperor still pressed onward, until he reached the Firth of Moray, and was struck with the difference in the length of the days, and shortness of the nights, compared with those in southern latitudes. Saving making a few new roads, and receiving the submission of the few tribes who chanced to lie in his way, he appears to have done nothing towards conquering this hardy race; so he returned to Newcastle, and began to build a stronger barrier than any of his predecessors had hitherto erected. On the northern side of this immense wall, he caused a deep ditch to be dug, about thirty-six feet wide, while the wall itself was twelve feet in height; thus, from the bottom of the ditch on the northern side there rose a barrier about twenty-five feet high, which was also further strengthened by a large number of fortifications, and more than three hundred turrets.

But before Severus had completed his gigantic labours, the Caledonians had again breached the more northern barrier, and fought their way up to the new trenches. The grey-headed old hero vowed vengeance, and swore by 'Mars the Red' that he would spare neither age nor sex. Death, who is sometimes merciful, kindly stepped in, and instead of allowing him to swing in his litter towards new scenes of slaughter, cut short his contemplated campaign at York, about the year 211; and after his death, the northern barrier was again given up to the Caledonians.

Hadrian's wall

A wearisome time must it have been to those Roman legions who had to keep guard on that long, monotonous wall, which went stretching for nearly seventy miles over hill and valley; nothing but a desolate country to look over, or that wide, yawning, melancholy ditch to peep into from the battlements, or a beacon-fire to light on the top of the turret, as a signal that the barbarians were approaching. An occasional skirmish must have been a relief to that weary round of everyday life, made up in marches from fort to fort, where there was no variety, other than a change of sentries – no relief excepting now and then sallying out for forage; for between the outer and inner wall, the whole country seems at this period to have been a wilderness – a silent field of death, in which the bones of many a brave man were left to bleach in the bleak wind, and from which only the croak of the raven and the howl of the wolf came upon the long dark midnights that settled down over those ancient battlements.

Sometimes the bold barbarians sailed around the end of the wall in their wicker boats, covered with black bull's hide, and landed within the Roman intrenchments, or spread consternation amongst the British villages; but with the exception of an occasional inroad like this, the whole of the northern part of the island appears to have been quiet for nearly another century, during which the Roman arms seem to have become weakened, while the British tribes became more interested in peace than war.

Such privileges as were granted to the Roman citizens were also now extended to the Britons; and under the dominion of Caracalla, the successor of Severus, there is little doubt that the southern islanders settled peaceably down in their homesteads, now comfortable abodes, and began to be somewhat more Romanized in their manners. Marriages took place between Romans and Britons, and love and peace now settled down side by side, in those very spots over which the rebellions of Cassivellaunus, Caractacus, and Boadicea had passed.

The wheels of the dreaded war-chariots seem to have rested on their axles; we scarcely meet with the record of a single revolt amongst the native tribes, excepting those beyond the wall of Hadrian. Through the pages of Gildas, we catch glimpses of strange miracles, and see the shadow of the cross falling over the old druidical altars, but nothing appears distinct; and although we may doubt many passages in the writings of this, our earliest historian, it would be uncharitable to the memory of the dead even to entertain a thought that he wilfully falsified a single fact. The only marvel is that living in an age when so few could write – when only common rumours were floating about him – when he was surrounded with the faint outlines of old traditions, he should have piled together so many facts which are borne out by contemporary history.

To place no faith in the narrative of Gildas is also to throw overboard the writings of the venerable Bede, and float over the sea of time for many a long year, without a single record to guide us. Although we have confidence in many of these ancient chronicles of the undefended dead, we shall pass on to undisputed facts, founded upon their faint records; for we have scarcely any other light to guide us through these dark caverns, which the ever-working hand of slow-consuming Time hath hollowed out.

*

Around the start of the fourth century, a new enemy made its appearance upon the British coast, and though it only at first flitted about from place to place like a shadow, it at last fixed itself firmly upon the soil, never again to be wholly obliterated. These were the Saxons – not at that period the only enemy which beside the Caledonians had invaded Britain, for there were others – Scandinavian pirates, always ready with their long ships to cross the British channel and raid along our coast.

These invaders were kept at bay for a time by a bold naval commander called Carausius, supposed himself originally to have been a pirate, and occasionally to have countenanced the inroads of the enemy; and on this account, or from the dreaded strength of his powerful fleet, a command was issued from Rome to put him to death.

The ruins of Richborough Castle, near Sandwich, Kent, one of the prime Roman sea-port defenses against attacks from Saxon pirates.

*A Carausius coin from Londinium mint.
On the reverse, the lion, symbol of Legio IV Flavia Felix.*

He, however, continued for some time to maintain mastery over the British Channel, defied Rome and all its powers, assumed the chief command over Britain, until he was at last stabbed by the hand of his own finance minister, Allectus, at York.

Allectus, Constantine, Chlorus, and Constantine the Great follow each other in succession, each doing their allotted work, then fading away into Egyptian darkness, scarcely leaving a record behind beyond their names; for the eyes of the Roman eagle were now beginning to wax dim, and a fading light was fast settling down upon the Eternal city, and gloomy and ominous shadows were ever seen flitting athwart the golden disc whose rounded glory had so long fallen unclouded upon Rome.

Even in Britain, the wall of Severus had been broken through, a Roman general slain, and London itself pillaged by hordes of barbarians. The plunderers were, however, attacked by Theodosius, the spoils retaken, and the inhabitants, whom they were driving before them in chains, liberated. These assailants are supposed to have been mingled bodies of the Picts, Scots, and Saxons, and the appellation 'Saxonicus' was added to the name of Theodosius, in honour of this victory.

The Roman soldiers in Britain now began to elect their own generals, and to shake off their allegiance to the Emperor. This was one undoubted cause for so few legions being found in England at this period, and a proof that that once mighty arm had already grown too weak to strike any effective blow in the distant territories. Chief amongst those elected to this high rank in Britain stood Maximus, who might doubtless have obtained undisputed possession of the British Island, had not his ambition led him to grasp at that portion of the Roman empire which was then in the possession of Gratian.

To accomplish this, he crossed over to Gaul with nearly all his island force, thus leaving Britain almost defenceless and at the mercy of the Picts, Scots, and Saxons, who were ever on the lookout for plunder. He attained his object, and lost his life, having been betrayed and put to death by Theodosius the Great, under whose sway the eastern and western empire of Rome was again united.

Alaric the Goth was now pouring his armed legions into Italy, and to meet this overwhelming force, Germany, Gaul and Britain were drained of their troops, and our island was again left a prey to the old invaders, who no doubt reaped another rich harvest; for the Britons, no longer able to defend themselves against these numerous hordes of barbarians, were compelled to apply for assistance to Rome.

Probably some time elapsed before the required aid was sent, for we cannot conceive that Stilicho would part with a single legion until after he had won the battle of Pollentia, and seen the routed army of Alaric in full retreat. Such was the penalty Britain paid for her progress in civilization – the flower of her youth were carried off to fight and fall in foreign wars; and when she most needed the powerful arms of her native sons to protect her, they were attacking the enemies of Rome in a distant land, and leaving their own island home a prey to new invaders.

Nor was this all: when the arms of Rome had grown too feeble to protect Britain – when beside their own legions, the country had been drained of almost every available soldier – when in every way it was weakened, and scarcely possessed the power to make any defence, it was deserted by the Romans, and left almost prostrate at the feet of Pictish, Scottish, and Saxon hordes, either to sue for mercy on the best terms that could be obtained, or to perish, from its very helplessness.

Alas! Rome could no longer defend herself, her glory had all but departed; and the Britons, who for about two centuries had never been allowed to defend themselves, and were now almost strangers to arms, were left to combat a force which many a time had driven back the Roman legions.

The few Roman troops that yet remained in Britain began to elect and depose their own commanders at pleasure.

They first chose Marcus, allowed him to rule for a short period, then put him to death.

Gratian was next elevated to power, bowed down to and obeyed for three or four months, then murdered.

Their next choice fell upon Constantine, influenced, it is said, by his high-sounding name; and it almost appears, by his carrying over his forces to Gaul, as Maximus had done before him, and aiming at a wider stretch of territory, that he scarcely thought Britain worth reigning over. Numbers of the brave British youth were sacrificed to his ambition; and England seems at this time to have only been a great nursery for foreign wars.

Gerontius, who appears to have been a British chief, now rose to some influence, and basely betrayed his countrymen by entering into a league with the Picts, Scots and Saxons, and no doubt sharing the plunder they took from the wretched Britons; he also appears to have carried an armed force out of the island, probably raised by means of the bargain he made with the barbarians.

He was pursued into Spain by the troops of the Roman emperor Honorius. He fled into a house for shelter after the battle; it was set fire to, and he perished in the flames – a dreadful death, yet almost merited by such a traitorous act as first selling his country to these northern robbers and pirates, carrying off those who were able to protect her, and then leaving his kindred a prey to the barbarians.

The Britons, in their misery, again applied for help to Rome. Honorius could render none, so he sent them such a letter as a cold friend, wearied out by repeated applications, sometimes pens to a poor, broken-down bankrupt; he could do nothing for them, they must now assist themselves; he forgave them the allegiance they owed, but had not a soldier to spare.

So were the Britons blessed with a liberty which was of no use to them; they were left to fend for themselves, like an old slave who instead of being a help, becomes an encumbrance to his taskmaster, who to get rid of him 'God blesses him,' and turns him out a free man, with the privilege to beg, or starve, or perish, unless in his old helpless age he can provide for himself.

Not that the Roman emperor was so unkind in himself. He would perhaps have assisted the Britons if he could; he was but one in a long chain of evils, and that the last, and least powerful, which, by disarming the Britons, and draining off all their strength to feed other channels, had reduced them to their present helpless state.

True, they had now temples, and baths, and pillared porticoes, and splendid galleries, and mosaic pavements, and beautifully shaped earthen-vessels; they had some knowledge of Roman literature, and, above all, Roman freedom. But alas! their old forest fortresses, and neglected war-chariots, and rude huts, guarded by the dangerous morass, and quaking bog, would now have stood them in better stead; their splendid mansions were but temptations to the barbarians, their broad, firm roads were so many open doors to the robbers. They may not inaptly be compared to some poor family, left in a large and splendid mansion in some dangerous neighbourhood, which the owner has deserted, with all his retinue and wealth, for fear of the thieves and murderers who were ever assailing him, leaving only behind a book or two for their amusement, a few useless statues to gaze upon, and but little beside great gaping galleries, whose very echoes were alarming to the new possessors.

Sir Walter Scott has beautifully said, when speaking of the Romans leaving the Britons in this defenceless state, that

> "Their parting exhortation to them to stand in their own defence, and their affectation of having, by abandoning the island, restored them to freedom, were as cruel as it would be to dismiss a domesticated bird or animal to shift for itself, after having been from its birth fed and supplied by the hand of man." [1]

Strange retribution, that whilst the sun of Rome should from this period sink never to rise again in its former glory, that of Britain should slowly emerge from the storm and clouds which threatened nothing but future darkness, and burst at last into a golden blaze, whose brightness now gilds the remotest regions of the earth.

But Britain had still a few sons left, worthy of the names which their brave forefathers bore. The blood of Boadicea still flowed in their veins; it might have been thinned by the luxury of the Roman bath, and deadened by long inactivity, but though it ran only sluggishly, it was still the same as had roused the strong hearts of Cassivellaunus and Caractacus when the Roman trumpets brayed defiance at the gates of their forest cities. There was still liberty or death left to struggle for; the Roman freedom they threw down in disdain, and trampled upon the solemn mockery; and when they once cast off this poisoned garment, they arose like men inspired with a new life.

They seemed to look about as if suddenly aroused from some despairing dream – as if astonished to hear their old island waves rolling upon a beach unploughed by the keel of a Roman galley – or as if wondering that they had not before broken through those circumscribed lines and forts and ramparts while they were yet guarded with the few Roman sentinels; they saw the sunshine streaming upon their broad meadows, and old forests and green hills and tall pale-faced cliffs, turning to gold every ripple that came from afar to embrace the sparkling sands of the white beach.

And they felt that such a beautiful country was never intended

---

1. Scott, W., *History of Scotland*, vol. i. p. 9.

1: Romano-British militiaman, 6th C
2: North British cavalryman, 6th C
3: Welsh tribal warrior, 5th-6th C

to become the home of slaves. They shed a few natural tears when they remembered how many of their sons and daughters had been borne over those billows in the gilded galleys of the invaders; they recalled the faces they had seen depart forever over the lessening waves; the mother weeping over her son; the manacled father, whose eyes burnt and throbbed, but had no tears; the pale-cheeked British maidens who sat with their faces buried in their hands as amid the distant sound of Roman music, their lovers were hurried away to leave their bones bleaching upon some foreign shore. They would have fallen down and prostrated themselves upon the ground for very sorrow, had not the thunder of their northern invaders rung with a startling sound in their ears, and they felt thankful that much work yet remained to be done, and that they were now left to fight their own battles, even as their forefathers had fought, in the dearly remembered days of their ancient glory.

With a population so thinned as it must have been by the heavy drainage made from time to time from the flower of its youth, we can readily conceive how difficult it was, after the departure of the Romans, to defend the wall which Severus had erected. But we cannot imagine that the Britons would hesitate to abandon a position which they could no longer maintain, or waste their strength at an outer barrier when the enemy had already marched far into the country.

On this point the venerable Gildas must have been misinformed, and the narrative of Zosimus is, beyond doubt, the correct one. From his history, it is evident that the Britons rose up and boldly defended themselves from the northern invaders; they also deposed the Roman rulers that still lingered in the British cities, and who, no longer overawed by the dictates of the emperor, doubtless hoped to establish themselves as kings, or chiefs, amongst the different tribes they had so long held in thrall.

But the Britons threw off this foreign yoke, and at last rooted out all that remained of the power of Rome. Besides the Picts and Scots, who were ever pouring in their ravaging hordes from the north, and the Saxons, who came with almost every favourable breeze which blew to the British shore, there was the old and stubborn foe to uproot, and one which had for four centuries retained a tenacious hold of our island soil.

Many of the Romans who remained were in possession of splendid mansions, and large estates, and as the imperial city was now over-run with bands of barbarians, they were loath to leave a land abounding with plenty, for a country then shaken to its very centre by the thunder of war. Though not clearly stated, there is strong reason to believe that these very Romans, who were so reluctant to quit Britain, connived at the ravages of the Picts and Scots, as if hoping, by their aid, once more to establish themselves in the island.

This was a terrible time for the struggling Britons. It was no longer a war in which offers of peace were made and hostages received, but a contest between two powers for the very soil on which they trod. This the islanders knew, and though often sorely depressed and hard driven, they still continued to look the storm in the face.

Every man had now his own household to fight for – the Roman party was led by Aurelius Ambrosius, and the British headed by Vortigern; a name which they long remembered and detested, for the misery it brought into the land.

As for Rome, she had no longer the leisure to turn her eye upon the distant struggle, for Attila and his Goths were now baying at her heels; there was a cry of wailing and lamentation in her towered streets, and the wide landscape which stretched at her imperial feet was blackened by the fire of the destroyer. She had no time, either to look on or send assistance to either party; and when Ætius had read the petition sent by the Britons, who complained that

> "the barbarians chase us into the sea; the sea throws us back upon the barbarians; and we have only the hard choice left us of perishing by the sword or by the waves,"

he doubtless cast it aside, and exclaimed:

"I also am beset by a host of enemies, and cannot help you."

A grim smile, perhaps, for a moment lit up his features, as he recalled the Romans who, false to their country, had lingered in the British island, and thus deserted him in Rome's hour of need; and as the stern shadow again settled down upon his features, he consoled himself for a moment by thinking that they, also, had met with their reward – and then again, he prepared to defend himself against the overwhelming force of Attila.

*

Harassed on all sides, the Britons now began to look to other quarters for aid, for they appear to have assembled at last under one head, and to have been guided in their course by Vortigern.

The character of this ancient British king is placed in so many various lights by the historians who have recorded the events of this obscure period that it is impossible to get at the truth. What he did is tolerably clear; nor are we altogether justified in ascribing his motives only to self advancement; pressed within and without by powerful enemies, he no doubt sought assistance from the strongest side, though it is not evident that he ever made any formal offer.

He must have had some acquaintance with the Saxons, whom he enlisted in his cause – it is improbable that he would hail an enemy, standing out at sea with his ships, and invite him to land and attack a foe with whom this very stranger had been allied. One man might have done so, but Vortigern's actions doubtless had the sanction of the British chiefs who were assembled around him at the time.

They must have had strong faith in the Saxons, and it is not improbable that some of them had been allowed to settle on the Isle of Thanet – they had already aided the Britons in their wars against the Romans, who were located in the island, as well as against their northern invaders, before they were intrusted with the defence of Britain.

But we must first glance at the England of that day before we introduce our Saxon ancestors – the 'grey forefathers' of our native land, whose very language outlived that of their Norman conquerors, and who blotted out almost every trace of the ancient Britons by their power.

As Sharon Turner says in his admirable history of the Anglo-Saxons, they were

> "A tribe which, in the days of Ptolemy, just darkened the neck of the peninsula of Jutland, and three inconsiderable islands in its neighbourhood. One of the obscure tribes whom Providence selected, and trained to form the nobler nations of France, Germany, and England, and who have accomplished their distinguished destiny."

These stand dimly arrayed upon the distant shore of time, and calmly await our attention.

7 BRITAIN AFTER THE ROMAN PERIOD

> What, though those golden eagles of the sun
> Have gone for ever, and we are alone,
> Shall we sit here and mourn? No! look around,
> There still are in the sky trails of their glory,
> And in the clouds traces where they have been. –
> Their wings no longer shadow us with fear.
> Let us then soar, and from this grovelling state
> Rise up, and be what they have never been.
>
> – *Ode to Hope*

Britain, after the departure of the Romans, was no longer a country covered every way with wild waving woods, dangerous bogs, and vast wastes of reedy and unprofitable marshes.

Smooth green pastures, where flocks and herds lowed and bleated, and long slips of corn waved in the summer sunshine, and fruit-trees which in spring were hung with white and crimson blossoms, and whose branches in autumn bowed beneath the weight of heavy fruitage, now swelled above the swampy waste, and gave a cheerful look to the grassy glade which had made room for the bright sunshine to enter into the very heart of those gloomy old forests.

Walled towns, also, heaved up above the landscape, and great broad brown roads went stretching for miles through a country over which, a few centuries before, a mounted horseman would have foundered. The dreamy silence which once reigned for weary miles over the lonesome woodland was now broken by the hum of human voices; and the ancient oaks, which for many a silent year had only over-shadowed the lairs of beasts of the chase, now overhung pleasant footpaths, or stretched along the sides of well-frequented roads, sure guides to the lonely wayfarer that he could no longer mistake his course from town to town.

Though many a broad bog, and long league of wood and wilderness still lay on either hand, yet, every here and there, the home of man rose up amid the waste, showing that the stir of life had begun to break the sleep of those solitudes. Instead of the shadowy avenue of trees which marked the entrance to their forest fortresses, lofty arches now spanned the roads which opened into their walled streets, and above the roofs of their houses tall temples towered in all the richness of Roman architecture, dedicated to the classical gods and goddesses whose sculptured forms graced the lofty domes of the imperial city.

Few and far between, in the dim groves whose silent shadows remained undisturbed, the tall grass climbed and drooped about the neglected altars of the druids, and on the huge stone where the holy fire once burned, the grey lichen and the green moss now grew. Even the Roman sentinel, as he paced to and fro behind the lofty battlement, sometimes halted in the midst of his measured march, and leaned on his spear to listen to the low 'Hallelujah' which came floating with faint sound upon the air, as if fearful of awakening the spirit of some angry idolator.

In the stars which pave the blue floor of heaven, men began to trace the form of the cross, and to see the spirit of the dove in the

white moonlight that threw its silver upon the face of the waters, for Britain already numbered amongst her slaughtered sons those who had suffered martrydom for the love they bore to their crucified Redeemer. Under the shadow of the Roman eagles had marched soldiers proud that they bore on their hearts the image of the cross of Christ. In spite of the decree of Diocletian, the Gospel sound still spread, and around the bleeding head of the British martyr St. Alban there shone a glory which eclipsed all the ancient splendour of Rome.

The mountains, the rivers, and the ancient oaks were soon to echo back the worship of the true God, and no longer to remain the objects of idolatry. The unholy doctrine of the druids was ere long to be unmasked – and instead of the gloomy gods which frowned down in stone amid the dark groves, and whose dead eyes ever looked upon the melancholy water that murmured around the altars on which they stood, the light of a benign countenance was about to break in beauty over the British isle, and a voice to be heard, proclaiming peace and good-will to all mankind.

For the Picts and Scots had already fallen back affrighted before the holy Hymns of Zion, and been more startled by the loud hallelujah chanted by the soldiers of Christ, who were led on by Germanus, than ever they were by the loud braying of the brazen trumpets of Rome.

British women, ever foremost to tread the paths of religion and virtue, had boldly heralded the way, and in spite of the glowering and forbidding looks of the druids, Græcina and Claudia had already knelt before the throne of the True God. Though the vanguard came heavily up amid cloud and storm, Hope, and Love, and Mercy rode fearlessly upon the wings of the tempest.

It is but just to the memory of those ancient Roman invaders, that we should confess that they never reduced to slavery and total subjection the tribes which they conquered. Generally, in return for the taxes they imposed, and the expense to which they put the invaded country, they instructed the inhabitants in the Roman arts – and although they humbled their martial spirit, and left the conquered tribes less able to defend themselves, still the signs of civilization everywhere marked their course.

Beside being brave generals, the Roman commanders were also able statesmen; nor had the Britons for centuries before, nor did they for centuries after, sleep in that peaceful security which they had enjoyed under the sway of the wise Agricola. Though the conquerors taxed their corn, they taught the Britons a better method of cultivating it; though they made heavy levies upon their cattle, they were the first to set them the example of reclaiming many an acre of pasturage from the hitherto useless marsh and forest. They instructed them in planting the fruit trees, from which the tithe was taken; and, in addition to orchards, pointed out to them the art of dressing vineyards. (Fifteen hundred years or more may have chilled our climate, but in those days, the purple and bunchy grape drooped around many a British homestead.)

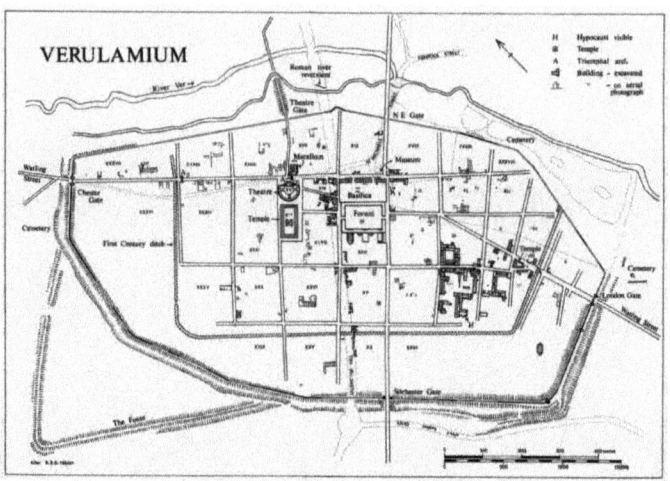

The chief towns were governed by Roman laws. London and Verulamium were already celebrated cities, and the latter reared high its lofty towers, temples, and theatres in all the architectural grandeur of Roman art. For centuries after did many of these majestic monuments remain, even when the skeleton of the once mighty Rome had all but crumbled into dust, as if to proclaim that the last work of those all-dreaded conquerors was the civilization of Britain.

They divided our island into five provinces, appointed governors and officers to administer justice, and collect taxes in each division. Over all these a chief ruler was placed, who was accountable for his actions to the Roman emperor, and whose written orders were given to him in a green-covered book, emblazoned with golden castles, when he was installed in the

dignity of his office – as, in almost all colonies, there were doubtless many who, 'clothed in authority,' ruled with an iron hand over their fellow men; not that such always escaped – for, as we have before stated, the revolt of Boadicea was caused by the oppression of Roman rulers, and the reckoning of her vengeance was truly dreadful.

We have already had occasion to remark how easily the Romans broke through the ancient British fortresses, and how frequently the Picts and Scots made inroads through the ramparts erected by the Romans. Saving, however, in such works as appear to have been hastily thrown up by the Britons, when they retreated into their native forests, they displayed considerable skill in the erection of their strongholds. They occasionally constructed high walls, with blocks of granite five or six feet long, and these they piled together without the aid of cement, digging a deep ditch outside, to make access more difficult; and as this fortress was built in the form of a circle, and the wall was of sufficient thickness to permit half a dozen men to walk on it abreast, it must, although not of such extent, have been as difficult to storm as the barriers thrown up by the Romans.

The huge stone, supposed to weigh upwards of seven hundred tons [*not the one illustrated above - ed.*], which is placed on the points of two rocks in Cornwall, and the massive blocks raised and piled on each other at Stonehenge show that ages before the Roman invasion, Britain was inhabited by a tribe whose knowledge of the power of leverage, and skill in removing such gigantic blocks from the distant quarries, were only surpassed by the builders of the Egyptian Pyramids.

No wonder, then, that a race possessed of such natural genius was, under the tuition of the Roman architects, able to produce such a class of workmen that there was demand for them even in Gaul; and that the skill of the British mechanic was in that early age acknowledged on the continent. Industry led to wealth, and the latter allowed for luxuries to which the simple Britons had, before the Roman period, been entire strangers; instead of the cloak of skin, and the dyed sagum, those who dwelt in towns now wore Roman togas.

British women began to decorate themselves with jewels of gold, silver, and precious stones, instead of their own island pearls, once so celebrated as to cause even a grave historian to attribute the invasion of Julius Cæsar to no other motive than a wish to fill his galley with them. They now wore bracelets and collars of gold, and amongst the imports to Britain, we find mention of ivory bridles, chains of gold, cups of amber, and drinking-vessels of glass, all made in the most elegant forms.

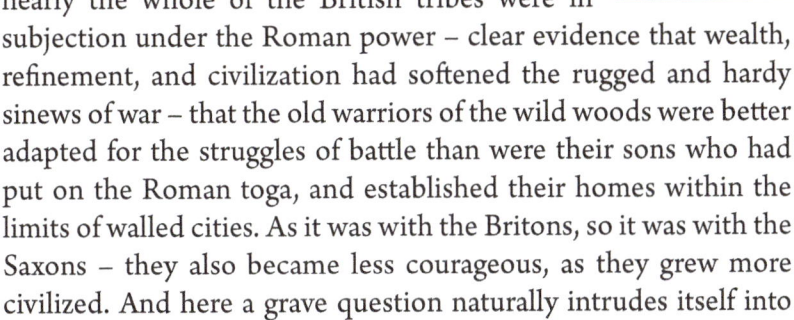

Great changes had taken place in the habits of these forest-dwellers, whose eyes in former days had seldom been gladdened by a sight of such treasures, unless when brought, now and then, by some warrior from the Gaulish wars, to be looked on and wondered at, or caught sight of for a moment amongst the coveted hoards of the druids. We have it on record that the waist of queen Boadicea was encircled by a chain, or girdle of gold; and shortly after we have proof that nearly the whole of the British tribes were in subjection under the Roman power – clear evidence that wealth, refinement, and civilization had softened the rugged and hardy sinews of war – that the old warriors of the wild woods were better adapted for the struggles of battle than were their sons who had put on the Roman toga, and established their homes within the limits of walled cities. As it was with the Britons, so it was with the Saxons – they also became less courageous, as they grew more civilized. And here a grave question naturally intrudes itself into our narrative, which to answer aright must either yield in favour of a state of barbarism, or pull down that great idol called a hero – though there are many exceptions on record to uphold the latter, some of which we have already mentioned, such as Cassivellaunus and Caractacus.

It is apparent that the more southern inhabitants of the British island had by this time adopted the Roman custom of interring their dead. Formerly the northern tribes did little more than place the body in the naked earth, cover it up, and mark the spot by a pile of stones; and that rude monument was left to point out the last resting-place of the departed.

The more southern tribes erected huge barrows above their dead, burying with them all that was considered most valuable, articles of gold and silver, weapons used in the war and in the chase, and even the body of the favourite dog, when he died, was considered worthy of sharing his master's grave. Many of these mounds of earth were immense, and in several cases it is clear that the soil which formed them had been brought from a considerable distance, perhaps from the very spot which had been marked by the valorous, though now forgotten, deeds of the dead.

These ancient sepulchres varied greatly in size and shape. Those which appear to have contained the remains of the earlier inhabitants of our island were frequently more than a hundred yards in length; and if, as it has been supposed, each follower brought his wicker basket of earth to empty upon the chieftain's grave, or the high-piled hillock was the work of the friends of the departed, though so many long centuries have elapsed, they yet speak of the respect in which those early warriors were held.

Sometimes the body was placed in a cist, with the legs drawn back towards the head This position of burial seems to have been adopted at a very remote period by the Britons. Sometimes the trunk of a large tree was cut up into a proportionate length, hewn hollow, and the body placed within it. This again appears to have been a custom of very ancient date.

They were also in the habit of burning the bodies of the dead – of collecting the burnt bones and placing them in the lowest bed of the barrow, then piling the stupendous mound above the ashes. Those tribes that became more Romanised appear to have followed the custom of their conquerors of burning the bodies, and collecting the ashes in urns; many of these have been discovered in what are called the Roman-British barrows, which display but indifferent workmanship. Others which have been dug out of old Roman burying-places show much elegance both in their forms and ornaments. With these have also been found mingled incense and drinking cups of the most beautiful patterns.

The Britons appear to have had no common graveyard; one barrow seems to have covered the remains of a chief, another that of his wife and children; perchance those who fell in the same battle were sometimes interred together, or it may be that the lesser hillocks covered the remains of the vassals, hemming around the huge barrow under which the chieftain slept, as if to protect him even in death – a silent guard surrounding his remains, as when living they had rallied about him.

What were the forms of their solemn processions – what ceremonies they used while burying their dead – what heathen prayers they offered up to their gods, or what war-hymns they chaunted over the remains of their chiefs, we know not. The snows of nearly 2,000 winters have fallen upon, their graves, but whether the latter were interred amid the deep war-cry of the tribe, or consigned to the earth amid tears and sorrowful sounds, we can never know. The glass beads, the amulets, and breastplates of gold – the spear-heads of bronze and flint, the rude necklaces of shells, and the pins and ornaments which we have discovered throw no light upon the name, rank, or history of the dead.

The barbarous custom of painting or tatooing their skins soon grew into disfavour as the Britons became civilized. They began to find other uses for the dye which they extracted from the herb called woad, and instead of distinguishing themselves by the hideous forms of beasts or reptiles which they were wont to puncture and imprint upon their bodies, they now bore the marks of their rank in the form of their costume, and sought for their renown in the plaudits of other men.

They began to look for their leaders amongst the ancient families, and to trace back their genealogies to their earliest heroes. This ended all Roman claims, for they refused to grant any land to such as had not descended from the primitive tribes; it led also to much dissension, to many heart-burnings and bitter jealousies; family was divided against family, and tribe against tribe; petty kings sprang up in every province; there was much blood shed – more to be spilt; and as Vortigern alone had maintained his claim, he was determined to support his position at any sacrifice.

Whether Hengist and Horsa came on a mission of peace, or as traders or pirates, or were driven by a storm upon the coast, or were exiled from their country, are matters of no importance. They were hired – their business was to fight, and they were paid for doing so. They accepted the terms offered by the British king, acquitted themselves manfully, and finally were the means of establishing the Saxons in Britain.

To the commencement of this period we have now arrived, and the next who pass through the gate of history are our English forefathers, the Saxons.

THE SAXON INVASION

8 THE ANCIENT SAXONS

> The stupendously holy gods considered these things:
> They gave names to the night and to the twilight;
> They called the morning and mid-day so.
> There sat an old man towards the east in a wood of iron,
> Where he nourished the sons of Fenris.
> Every one of these grew up prodigious – a giant form,
> – The sons of the two brothers inhabit
> The vast mansions of the winds.
> A hall stands brighter than the sun,
> Covered with gold in Gimle."
>
> – *The Volupsa*

The Saxons were a German or Gothic race, possessing an entirely different language to that of the Celts or ancient Britons; and although they do not appear to have attracted the same attention as the other tribes, they were, doubtless, settled at a very early period in Europe. At the time when they begin to stand forth so prominently in the pages of history, they occupied the peninsula of Jutland, now a portion of Denmark, with two or three neighbouring islands, known by the names of North Strande, Busen, and Heligoland, all situated near the mouth of the Elbe.

As they, however, consisted of three tribes – namely, the Jutes, the Angles, and the Saxons – they probably, at a former period, stretched over a much larger surface of country, the boundaries of which are now difficult to define. As early as the time of Ptolemy, a branch of this ancient Scythian race was known as the Saxons. They claimed their descent from Odin, probably some old and celebrated warrior, whose deeds grew up under magnified traditions, until at last he was dignified with the title of a god.

Like the Britons, they were a brave and fearless race, delighting in plunder and slaughter, ever choosing the most dangerous and perilous paths, loving the roll of the wave, and the roar of the storm, and generally landing under a gloomy and tempestuous sky, to surprise and attack the enemy. Their arms were a sharp sword, a keen-pointed dagger, a tall spear, and a ponderous battle-axe, all made of good iron. But the most dreaded weapon they wielded seems to have been a large heavy hammer, from which projected a number of sharp-pointed spikes. This fearful instrument was the terror of their enemies, and no helmet was proof against its blows.

Their chiefs wore a kind of scaly armour, which appears to have been formed of iron rings, locked together upon a tight-fitting coat, or leathern doublet. The rims and bosses of their shields were of iron, while the body was sometimes formed of wood, and covered with leather. Many of these shields were large enough to protect the whole form, and as they were convex, no doubt the point of the enemy's weapon would glide off, unless it was struck firmly into the centre; thus they formed a kind of moveable bulwark, behind which the warrior sheltered himself in battle.

They believed that the souls of those who bravely perished on the hard-fought field were at once wafted into the halls of Valhalla, and the terrible heaven which they pictured in a future state consisted of those dreadful delights so congenial to their brutal natures while on earth – being made up of a succession of conflicts and struggles, cleaving of helmets and hacking of limbs; and that when the twilight deepened over those awful halls, every warrior was again healed of his wounds; that they then sat down to their grim and hideous banquet, where they fed upon a great boar, whose flesh never diminished, however much they ate, and when they had satiated themselves with these savoury morsels, which they cut off with their daggers, they washed them down with deep draughts of mead, which they drank out of the skulls of their cowardly enemies.

upon her hard bed, and dark Delay kept watch against the sombre doors which she never opened. Such were the eternal abodes those barbarians believed they should enter after death – the realms which their stormy spirits would soar into, when they could no longer guide their barks over the shadows of the overhanging rocks – when the tempestuous sea no longer bore them upon the thunder of its billows, and cast them upon some distant coast, to revel in carnage and slaughter – it was then that they turned their dying eyes to the coveted halls of Valhalla, and that huge banquet-table on which the grisly boar lay stretched, surrounded by drinking-cups formed of human skulls.

Those who had not the courage sufficient to win an entrance into these envied realms by their own bravery put one of their slaves to death, in the belief that such a sacrifice was acceptable to

Odin, and a sure passport into this ideal world.

They, however, also believed that Valhalla would at last pass away; that Odin himself perish; and that the good and the brave would inhabit another heaven, called Gimle.

The evil and the cowardly would be consigned to a more awful place of punishment than that over which Hela reigned. The gods would sit in judgment, and Surtur, the black one, would appear, and an evil spirit be liberated from the dark cave in which he had been for ages bound with chains of iron. For three years, increasing snow would fall from all quarters of the world, and during this long winter there would be no summer, neither would any green thing grow, but all mankind would perish by each other's hands.

Then two huge monsters would appear, one of which would devour the sun and the other the moon. The mountains and trees would be torn up, and the earth shaken to its deepest foundations. The stars would be blotted out of heaven, and one wide shoreless sea would cover the whole world, over which a solitary ship would float, built of the nails of dead men, and steered by the tall giant Hrymer. Then would the huge wolf Fenris open his enormous mouth, the lower jaw of which would touch the earth, and the upper the heavens, over which a serpent would breathe poison, while the sons of Muspell rode forward, led by the black Surtur. A blazing fire, spreading out its myriad tongues of flame, would burn before and behind him; his sword would glitter like the sun, and the bridge which spanned across heaven would be broken.

Towards a large plain would these terrible forces move, followed by Fenris, the wolf. The brazen trumpet of Heimdal

would ring out such a startling peal as would awaken the gods, and cause the mighty ash of Ygdrasil to tremble. Odin would put on his golden helmet, and all the gods rise up in arms, and after the wolf had devoured him, and its jaws had been rent asunder by Vidar, the whole universe would be destroyed.

*

Such a creed as this was calculated to nourish and keep alive the most benighted superstitions amongst its believers. Thus we find them drawing omens from the flight and singing of birds, placing their trust in good and evil days, and considering the full or new moon as the most favourable seasons during which to put into operation any important plan. They were influenced by the moving of the clouds, and directed by the course of the winds; and from the entrails of sacrificed victims they drew their auguries. The breastplates they wore were imperfect unless the smith who forged them muttered a charm while he wielded his ponderous hammer. Even the graves of dead men were frequented, and those who slept their last sleep were entreated to answer them. They predicted the outcome of a battle by seizing an enemy, and compelling him to fight with one of their own race. From the branches of the oak they cut short twigs, marked them, then scattered them at random upon a white garment, and while the priest looked upward, he took those on which his hand chanced to alight, and if they proved to be those on which the favourite mark was impressed, it was considered a good omen.

They rode out the perilous tempest on the deep with better heart if, on the departure of their bark from the stormy beach, some priestess, with her hair blown back, stood upon the giddy headland and chanted the mystic rhyme which they believed would waft them, more safely than the most favourable breeze, to the distant shore. Even through the long night of time we can picture her standing upon the edge of the rock, while the white-winged sea-gull wheeled and screamed above her head; with the subdued thunder of the hoarse waves ever rolling at her feet, her drapery blown aside, and her wan and thin lips moving; while the sailors, tugging at their long oars with their brawny arms and bowed heads, sent up a silent prayer to the god of the storm.

Such were our forefathers – men who would startle at the stirring of a leaf, or the shooting of a star, yet who were brave enough to rush upon the point of a spear with a flushed cheek and a bright eye, and who could look death full in the face without a feeling of fear. Nor would it be difficult to point out, even in our own day, numbers of superstitious signs and omens, which are as

implicitly believed in by the peasantry of the present age, as they were by the ancient Saxons during this dark period of our history. The chattering of a magpie, the croaking of a raven, the howling of a dog in the night, a winding-sheet in the candle, or a hollow cinder leaping out of the fire upon the hearth, are even now held amongst our superstitious countrymen as ominous of ill-luck, sickness, or death. Scarcely an obscure English province is without its wise-man, or cunning fortune-teller; those lingering remains of the Wicca of the Saxons, which have descended to us through nearly two thousand years, in spite of the burnings and other executions which were so common in our country only two or three centuries ago, when not to believe in witchcraft would have been held a crime equal to atheism by our more enlightened and comparatively modern forefathers.

The temple erected to their war-god, in their own country, appears to have been spacious and magnificent. On the top of a marble column stood this idol, in the figure of a tall, armed warrior, bearing a banner in his right hand, on which a red rose was emblazoned, while in his left he held a balance. His helmet was surmounted with a cock; on his breastplate a bear was engraven, while on the shield which was suspended from his shoulder was the image of a lion, upon a ground of flowers. Here, women divined, and men sacrificed, and into the battle was this warlike

image borne by the priest; for as they could not trust themselves upon the sea without a charm being first muttered, so in the field did they require the image of their idol to countenance the contest. To this grim deity did they offer up their captives, and even those of their own tribe who had fled, and turned their backs upon the fight, for they looked upon cowardice as the greatest of crimes amongst their men, and wantonness in their women they punished with death.

Some of their idols are surrounded by a wild poetry, and an air of almost classic beauty, recalling to the mind the divinities worshipped by the ancient Greeks and Romans. Of such was their goddess, called the Mother of Earth, who was held so sacred that only the priest was permitted to touch her. Her temple stood among the solemn shadows of a silent grove; her figure was always covered by a white garment which was washed in a secret lake; in those waters the slaves who administered at her shrine were drowned – no one, saving the priest, was allowed to go abroad, who were once entrusted with her mysteries. On holy days her image was borne in procession, on the backs of beautifully marked cows. Nothing but joy and peace then reigned throughout the whole length and breadth of the land: the bark was moored upon the beach; the spear and battle-axe hung upon the beam above the hearth, and Odin himself seemed to sleep.

But this lasted no longer than the days allotted to these processions: when they had passed, the keel was again launched, the weapons taken from their resting-place, while grim-visaged war resumed his wrinkled front.

Even the cattle that fed upon the island where this temple stood were held so sacred that it was a crime to touch them, and he who drew water from the fountain that flowed beside the grove, dared not, even by a whisper, disturb the surrounding silence. We might almost fancy, while reading the description of the idol they named Crodus, that we saw before us the embodiment of one of Spenser's beautiful stanzas, or that he himself had but turned into verse some old record, in which he found pictured this image of one of the ancient Saxon gods. It was of the figure of an old man, stooping through very age: he was clothed in a white garment; a girdle of linen, the ends of which hung loose, encircled his waist; his head was grey, and bare. He held in his right hand a vessel, in which flowers floated in water; his left hand rested upon a wheel, while he stood with his naked feet upon the back of a prickly perch. How like Spenser's description is the above, of his "Old January wrapped well in many weeds, to keep the cold away – of February, with the old waggon-wheels and fish – of the hand cold through holding all the day the hatchet keen." Such a resemblance would the eye of a poet trace, and so would he transform old Crodus, the Saxon idol, into the personification of one of his months.

Whoever broke into one of their temples, and stole the sacred vessels, was punished with a slow, lingering, and terrible death. To the very edge of the sands of the sea-shore he was dragged, when the tide was low, and there made fast. His ears were cut off, and other parts of his body mutilated – then he was left alone. Wave after wave came and went, and washed around him, as the tide came in; he felt the sea rising every minute, inch by inch – higher still, higher it came – every ripple that made a murmur on the shore rang his death-knell, until the last wave came that washed over him – then vengeance was satisfied. A more awful death can scarcely be imagined.

*

They were a tall, big-boned, blue-eyed race of men, and it appears from an old law made to punish a man who seized another by the hair, that they at one period wore it so long as to fall upon the shoulders. The females wore ornaments on their arms and necks.

The government was generally vested in the hands of the aged, and they appear to have elected their ruler in war by the chiefs assembling and drawing lots. He on whom it fell, they followed and obeyed; but when the war was over, they were again all equal. They were divided into four orders – the Etheling, or noble, who never married below his own rank; the free-man, who shared in the offices of government; the freed-man, or he who, either by purchase or merit, had obtained his liberty; and the serf, or slave.

They reckoned their time by the number of nights, and counted their years by the winters. April they named Easter month, after their goddess, Eostre. Thus we still retain a name which, though commemorating the worship of an ancient idol, has now become endeared to us by the Resurrection of Christ – a holy time which we can never forget, for at every return it seems to bring back a spirit of beauty into the world, whose pathway is strewn with the sweetest and earliest flowers of spring. Bright spots of light every way break through this age of barbarism, and May, which again hangs the snow-white blossoms upon the hawthorn, they called the milk-month; nor can we now repeat the name without images of lowing cattle and pleasant pastures springing up before us, and we marvel how so warlike a race ever came to make use of such poetical and pastoral names. The sun they worshipped as a goddess; the moon as a god. A Saxon poet would have called the former 'the golden lady of the day.'

Although they appear to have been ignorant of the use of letters, yet there is but little doubt that they used certain signs, or characters, which they were able to interpret. Some of these Runic hieroglyphics seem to have been engraved on their swords. Their war-songs were committed to memory, and it is probable that many a one ranked high amongst their minstrels who possessed no other talent than that of remembering and repeating these ancient lays. It might be that they were just enabled to form characters clear enough in their resemblance to some natural object, which,

Anglo-Saxon runes

when inscribed upon the rugged monumental stone, bore some allusion to the name or bravery of the chief whose memory it perpetuated. Their only books seem to have been the bark of trees; the rind of the beech their favourite register; a tablet on which the rustic chronicler of the present day still makes the mark of his fair one's name, in characters only legible to himself.

In point of civilization, they were at this time centuries behind the Britons, and an old author, describing them about the fifth century, says,

> "You see amongst them as many piratical leaders as you behold rowers, for they all command, obey, teach, and learn the art of pillage. Hence, after your greatest caution, still greater care is requisite. This enemy is fiercer than any other; if you be unguarded, they attack; if prepared, they elude you. They despise the opposing, and destroy the unwary; if they pursue, they overtake; if they fly, they escape. Shipwrecks discipline them, not deter; they do not merely know, they are familiar with, all the dangers of the sea; a tempest gives them security and success, for it divests the meditated land of the apprehension of a descent. In the midst of waves and threatening rocks they rejoice at their peril, because they hope to surprise."
>
> "Dispersed into many bodies," adds Zosimus, "they plundered by night, and when day appeared, they concealed themselves in the woods, feasting on the booty they had gained."

When the Saxons first approached the British coast, they issued out from the mouth of the Elbe, in wicker boats covered with leather, which seem to have been but little better than the coracles used by the ancient Britons. These were so light that they found but little difficulty in carrying them overland from one river or creek to another, then paddling their way under cover of the banks, wherever sufficient water was to be found, until at last they came unaware upon the natives.

The chiules or keels which they possessed at the time they were called upon to aid Vortigern were capable of carrying more than a hundred men each, a wonderful improvement on the frail barks with which they first ventured into the British seas. Such as we have here described them, were the tribe destined to overthrow an ancient race, whom the Romans never wholly subjugated.

9 HENGIST, HORSA, ROWENA AND VORTIGERN

> They bargained for Thanet with Hengist and Horsa,
> Their aggrandizement was to us disgraceful,
> After the destroying secret
> with the slaves at the confluent stream,
> Conceive the intoxication at the great banquet of Mead,
> Conceive the deaths in the great hour of necessity;
> Conceive the fierce wounds – the tears of the women –
> The grief that was excited by the weak chief (Vortigern);
> Conceive the sadness that will be revolving to us,
> When the brawlers of Thanet shall be our princes.
>
> – Ancient Welsh poem, seventh century

We have no account of the preliminary arrangements between the British king and the Saxon chiefs, when the latter arrived with three ships, and landed at Ebbs-fleet, a spot which now lies far inland, though at that period the Wanstum was navigable by large vessels, and formed a broad barrier between the Island of Thanet and the mainland of Kent.

Vortigern and his chieftains were assembled in council when the Saxons appeared, and Hengist and Horsa were summoned before them. The Saxon ships, which contained about three hundred soldiers, were drawn up beside the shore, where the adventurers anxiously awaited the outcome of the interview between their leaders and the British king. Such a meeting as this could scarcely result from chance; the time of landing – the assembled council – the attendance of Hengist and Horsa, all bear evidence of some previous understanding between the parties, similar to what we have before alluded to.

LANDING OF HENGIST AND HORSA.

Vortigern first interrogated the Saxons as to the nature of their creed; Hengist enumerated the names of the gods they worshipped, and further added that they also dedicated the fourth and sixth days in the week to Woden and Frea. Inference might be drawn from the reply of Vortigern, that the Britons were already Christians, though such a conclusion ought, doubtless, to be limited in its application to the inhabitants of our island, for we have evidence that all were not.

It was agreed that the Saxons were to assist the Britons, to drive the Scots and Picts out of the island – and that for such service they were to receive food and clothing, and when not engaged in war they were to be stationed in Ruithina, for by that name was the Isle of Thanet then called by the ancient Britons. [Thanet is no longer an island – *ed.*]

There is no evidence that Vortigern intended to give up this island, at that period, to the Saxons; the arrangement he made had nothing new in it. Centuries before, the Britons had crossed the sea, and fought in the wars of the Gauls; they had also aided the Romans: it was a common custom for one nation to hire the

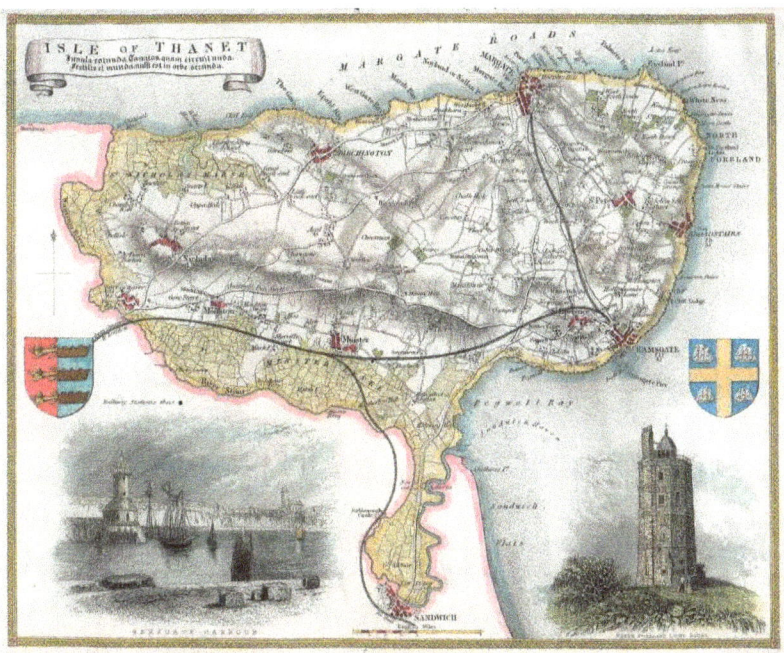

assistance of another; when the time of service was over, the soldiers either returned to their own country, or settled down amongst the native tribes, whom they had defended - as in Britain, many of the Romans and Gauls had done beforehand.

In this case, however, the result proved very different, though it would have been difficult for any one endowed with even the keenest penetration to have foreseen that three small ships, probably containing in all not more than three hundred men, and these willing to render assistance on very humble terms, should point out a way over the waves, by which their companions in arms should come, and conquer, and take possession of a country which it had cost the Romans so many years of hard warfare to subjugate.

The Saxons appear to have done their duty. Fighting was their every-day trade: their robust natures had received no touch of Roman refinement. They earned their bread with the points of their swords and the blows of their heavy battle-axes; they drove back the northern hordes beyond the Roman walls, and so they soon grew into great favour with the Britons. All this was very natural to a nation now making rapid progress in civilization, and one wealthy enough to pay others for fighting its battles – it was a much easier life to sit comfortably in their walled cities, to follow the chase, and enjoy the luxury of the bath, than to be chasing the Picts and Scots from one county to another, through forests and morasses, and over hills and dales, day after day; but to do this securely, more aid was required.

Hengist and Horsa had left numbers of their countrymen behind, who would willingly fight on the same terms which they had accepted. Vortigern agreed to the proposition they made, and more Saxons were speedily sent for. Seventeen ships soon arrived, and on the deck of one of these vessels, from the stern of which the banner of the white horse waved, stood a conqueror whose long silken locks blew out in the breeze, unencumbered by either helmet or crest, who bore neither sword, spear, shield nor battle-axe, but was armed only with a pair of beautiful blue eyes, and a face of such strange and surpassing beauty as had never before been mirrored in our island  waves: such was the Saxon Princess Rowena, destined to win more broad acres from the Britons without striking a single blow, than all the northern barbarians had ever gained by their numberless invasions.

On the landing of his daughter, accompanied by so many of her countrymen, a great feast would, of course, be held to celebrate the event, and there Vortigern and the British chiefs would, beyond doubt, be assembled to welcome their new allies; there is nothing remarkable in such an occurrence, nor in Rowena drinking to her father's royal guest, nor in the island king falling at once in love with the beautiful barbarian. Her drinking his health in a tongue to

which he was a stranger, her natural bashfulness, on first standing in the presence of the British king – her confusion when she found her language was not understood by him – all, doubtless, contributed to make her look more interesting.

Then above all to know that the blood of Woden flowed in her veins, that she had descended from a hero, whose renown in battle had raised him to the grandeur of a god, in the idolatrous estimation of his own countrymen; all these things coupled together had surely romance and poetry enough about them, aided by such a beautiful countenance, to turn a calmer brain than Vortigern's, heated as his was by love and wine.

Vortigern and Rowena

He had no peace until he married her; her image seems to have haunted his memory, and caused him more uneasiness until she became his wife, than all the inroads of the northern hordes had hitherto done. Even before this period, all had gone on smoothly and evenly between the Britons and the Saxons; but now Love himself had landed amongst the last-comers, and received the warmest welcome of them all. Who could dream that he but heralded the way for slaughter, conquest, and death to follow in, or that the beauty he accompanied should be the cause of bloodshed between the Saxons and the Britons? – yet so it was.

The Saxons were, shortly after, the sole possessors of the isle of Thanet, and the influence of Vortigern's pretty pagan wife was soon visible to the jealous eyes of the Britons. Hengist and Horsa began to demand more liberal supplies, and to cast a longing glance upon Kent; but the Britons had spirit enough to resist such a concession, and here we for a time lose sight of Vortigern and Rowena, though it is highly probable that they retreated into the isle of Thanet, then held by the Saxons, from the coming storm.

Vortimer and Catigern, the two sons of Vortigern by a former marriage, now took the command of the Britons, with whom the Roman settlers in the island appear to have joined; all resolved to unite, and to drive the Saxons out of Britain. Hengist and Horsa, to strengthen their force, formed a league with their old brothers in plunder, the Scots and Picts, and war once more broke out in the land, more terrible in its results than it had ever been in the struggles between the Britons and the Romans.

What few fragments we find in the old Welsh bards alluding to these ancient battles, are filled with dreadful descriptions, and awful images of slaughter. We are borne onward, from the shout of the onset, to the mighty shock when the opposing ranks close in battle, when blade clashes against blade, when dark frowning men sink with gory seams on their foreheads, and tall chieftains rock and struggle together in the combat, and as each knee is brought to the ground, it rests upon a bed of gore, while battle-axes, as they are uplifted, and glitter a moment in the air, rain down endless streams of blood.

Then gloomy biers pass by, on which 'red-men' are borne; and ravens come sweeping through the dim twilight which settles over that ancient battlefield, to prey upon the fallen warriors. Such wailings as these must have caused the heart of Vortigern beat painfully, even when the fair head of Rowena was pillowed upon it, and to have made him sigh, and regret that such beauty had been purchased at so great a sacrifice.

At the battle of the Ford-of-Eagles, long after called Eaglesford, but now Aylesford, in Kent, Horsa, the brother of Hengist, fell; he whose banner of the white-horse had waved over many a victorious field, and been the terror of the northern tribes, now fell to rise no more. On the side of the Britons also perished Catigern, and a sore reproach must his death have been to his father, Vortigern, when he heard the tidings! For, alas, he was wasting the hours in soft dalliance with his blue-eyed idolater, while his sons were fighting and falling in defence of their country.

Vortimer had now the sole command of the Britons, and, if the ancient bards are to be believed, it was by his hand that Horsa was slain. A sad pang must such a rumour as this have sent through the aching heart of poor Rowena, as she gazed upon her husband, and in him beheld the father of her uncle's murderer, the destroyer of her father's companion in arms – he who had shared the fortunes of Hengist, from the hour when first the prow of their ship ploughed together the sands on the British shore.

One of our old chroniclers – Roger de Wendover – states that, on a future day, Rowena bitterly revenged the death of Horsa, by bribing one of Vortimer's servants to poison her son-in-law, and that thus fell, in the bloom of life, one of the noblest of the British warriors – a victim to the vengeance of his step-mother. Whether this is true or not, it is now impossible to decide, so much are the statements of our early historians at variance; one thing, however, is clear – the Saxons were defeated, and compelled to escape in their long chiules, or ships; nor do they appear to have returned until after the death of Vortimer, when, at the suggestion of Rowena, her father was again invited to Britain, and this time Hengist returned with a larger force than had hitherto landed in our island.

When the Saxon landed, he made an offer of peace to the Britons, and invited the chiefs to a feast, which he gave on the occasion. Both parties were to come without their arms, such was the command issued by Hengist, and enforced on the part of the British leaders by Vortigern, who was also present.

The treacherous Saxon had, however, given orders to his followers to conceal short swords or daggers under their garments, and when he gave the signal, to fall upon and slaughter every Briton present, with the exception of Vortigern.

The feast commenced, the wine-cup circulated, the Saxon and British chiefs sat side by side; those who had fought together, face to face and hand to hand, were drinking from the same cup, for it appears to have been so contrived that a false friend should be placed between every foe. Vortigern seems to have sat secure, and never once dreamed of the treachery that surrounded him; and, perhaps, even before the smile had well faded from Hengist's face, as he talked of the pleasant days that were yet in store for his unsuspecting son-in-law, he turned round and exclaimed: "Nimed eure saxes" – "unsheath your swords" – and a few moments later, three hundred British chiefs and nobles lay lifeless upon the ground.

The motto prefixed to our present chapter is from one of the poems of Golyddan, a Welsh bard, who lived within a century or two after this cold-blooded massacre, a deed which must for many a long year afterwards have rankled in the minds of the Britons, and which their bards would never allow to slumber, whenever they sang the deeds of their departed chieftains.

Doubtless Rowena was present at that bloody banquet, and with a cruel look confronted 'the weak chief,' as he stood pale and horror-stricken, glancing from father to daughter, and cursing the hour, as he looked into the face of the

beautiful heathen, whose blue eyes could perchance gaze, without shrinking for a moment, upon those wan and clay-cold countenances that were now upturned in death.

Though long years have passed away, and the hawthorns have put out their blossoms more than a thousand times since the fatal May in which this terrible tragedy took place, still the eye of the imagination can scarcely conjure up the scene without a shiver.

It is supposed to have been near Stonehenge where this cruel butchery took place, probably within the very circle of those Druid monuments, some of which still stand, though at that period the whole temple was, doubtless, perfect.

If, as we are led to believe, many of the British chieftains were Christians, there was something in keeping with the stern character of the Saxon pagans, in thus slaughtering their enemies in the presence of the very altars on which the islanders had formerly sacrificed to the gods they themselves worshipped, and such an act might, in their eyes, hallow even this savage revenge.

To slaughter all who did not believe in their heathen creed, was with the pagan Saxons a religious duty; they believed such acts were acceptable to their gods.

We shudder at the very thought of such a deed – nearly fourteen centuries have elapsed since the sands of Salisbury Plain drank in the blood of these victims. Yet we startle to see the dead thus piled together around the grey old stones which the footsteps of Time have all but worn away, as if we still looked calmly on while they were brought bleeding to our very thresholds. Still the historian of the past might mingle his sympathy, and carry back many a deed which has since then been done, to be rolled up and mourned over in the same great catalogue of cruelty.

The shadows that move through the old twilight of time bend under the weight of the 'red-men' that are borne upon the bier. The form of Hengist seems to stand leaning upon the red pillars that mark the entrance to the Hall of Murder in Valhalla, as if wondering "why the chariot wheels so long delayed," and the guests that still tarried behind, hastened to the banquet of skulls, which stood awaiting their coming, in the halls of Odin. For such a deed stamps him as a fitting servitor in that horrible hall of slaughter.

*

At Crayford in Kent, another great battle was fought between the Saxons and the Britons, in which the latter were defeated with great slaughter, and so complete was the victory, that the remnant of the British army were compelled to retreat into London.

But with all his success, Hengist was unable to keep possession of little more than the county of Kent and the island of Thanet, and even this, it appears, he would have found it difficult to retain, but for the dissensions which were ever breaking out amongst the British chiefs.

The Britons were able at this very time to send out twelve thousand armed men into Gaul, to war against the Visigoths, so that there can be but little doubt that, had unity reigned amongst them, they would have found no difficulty in driving out the Saxons, as they had done previouslye. The island seems to have been so divided at this period, and under the command of so many

different chiefs or kings, that they cared not to bring their united forces to bear upon one corner of the kingdom, especially that where the presence of Vortigern still appears to have been acknowledged; for it is probable that the British king, after the death of his son, settled down in his old age, amongst the Saxons, "a sadder and a wiser man."

We even hope, in spite of his misdeeds, and the miseries into which his love for a fair face plunged the whole island of Britain, that there is no truth to the statements of our early Saxon historians, who have left it on record that he fled into Wales, where, hated alike "by slave and free-man, monk and layman, strong and weak, small and great," he at last perished with the fair Rowena, and all his family, in the flames which destroyed the fortress where he had sought shelter from his enemies.

Yet many venerable names might be brought forward in support of this story of the terrible end of an ancient British king. A dreadful fate for fair Rowena, if true, and all the evidence is sadly in its favour, and from our hearts, we cannot help pitying the poor girl, who with downcast eyes, as she held the golden goblet in her hand, listened to the promises which the island monarch poured into her ears; who stepped from the deck of her father's galley, to share a throne, yet appears never to have forsaken her husband in all the varied vicissitudes of his chequered life; but through battle, flood, and fire, to have trod the same perilous path with him, hand in hand, sometimes, it may be, when alone, shedding tears at the remembrance of her father's cruelties, weeping one hour, for the death of her own friends, and the next, comforting Vortigern for the loss of those he mourned.

We picture her, as in the joyousness of her heart she left her native home to meet her father – no mother appears to have accompanied her – and, pagan as she was, we know not how pure and holy the feelings of that heart might be; for, red with blood as the hands of Hengist were, they had, doubtless, many a time parted her silken ringlets, as he stooped down and imprinted a father's kiss upon her. Perhaps a tear stole down the deep furrows which time and care had ploughed in the weather-beaten countenance of Hengist, as he embraced her when she first landed on our island shore, as in her pure countenance he traced the image of her mother, whom he had once so fondly loved.

Poor Rowena! She might have moved like a ministering angel, through all the terrors of those stormy times, her mild blue eyes beaming comfort on every woe-begone countenance on which they glanced – now soothing the restless slumber of her father, as he started up, dreaming of some new revenge, and by her falling tears, and low-breathed whispers, chasing away the dark demon from his couch; for even through the past, those gentle eyes seem to beam upon us, and the tears by which they are dimmed quench the cruel light, that when in anger, flashed from beneath her fringed eye-lids.

Oh, Mercy! Do not leave that beautiful Saxon mother to perish shrieking amidst the surrounding flames! What crimes she had

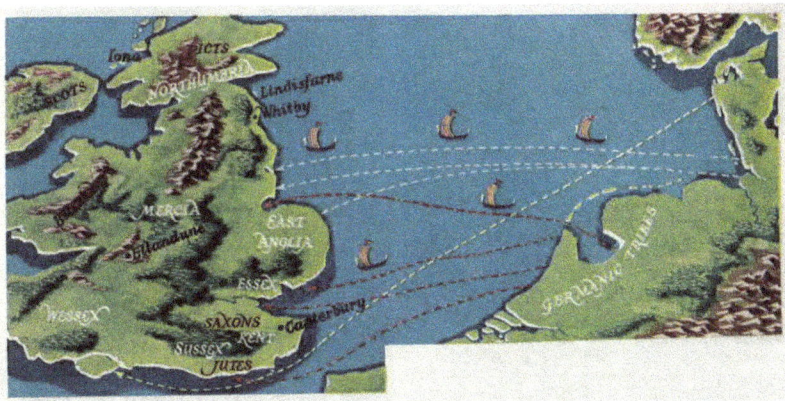

sprang from her faith; she was nursed in a cruel creed; when the grim shadow of Odin fell not over and darkened her gentle heart, she was a fond woman, even as our mothers have ever been. But she is dead and gone.

Hengist is now no more, and Eric, his son, reigns sole king over the white cliffs, green hills, and pastoral valleys of Kent, and the keels of other boats are grating upon our chalky headlands. The grey curtain of Time again drops down over the dead which in fancy stood before us, and after the night of death is past, a new morning breaks, that "laughs aside the clouds with playful scorn."

10 ELLA, CERDRIC, AND KING ARTHUR

He was a shield to his country:
The courteous leader of the army;
His course was a wheel in battle,
He was a city to old age;
The head, the noblest pillar of Britain;
An eagle to his foe in his thrust,
Brave as generous;
In the angry warfare, certain of victory.

– *Llywarch Hen., Sixth Century*

The next Saxon chieftain of any note who made a landing in Britain and established himself in the country was Ella. He came accompanied by his three sons and the same number of ships, the latter being anchored beside the Isle of Thanet, where Hengist and Horsa, 28 years before, had become auxiliaries under Vortigern.

From the south of Kent, a vast forest extended into Sussex and Hampshire, a huge uncultivated wilderness, called Andreade, or Andredswold, measuring above a hundred miles in length, and a long day's march in breadth, for it was full thirty miles wide, and abounded with wolves, deer, and wild boars.

Near the Sussex entrance of this primeval English forest, Ella fought his first battle, and drove the Britons into the wide wooded waste. After a time, the Saxon chief received fresh reinforcements, and not until then did he venture to attack the ancient British town which was named Andredes Ceaster, and stood, strongly fortified, on the edge of the forest. While the Saxons were attempting to scale the walls, a body of the Britons rushed upon them from the wood, and, thus attacked in the rear, the invaders were compelled to turn away from the town and carry the fight into the forest.

Three times was the assault renewed, for no sooner were the Saxons at the foot of the wall than the Britons were upon their heels. Each time, Ella's loss was severe; night came, and both parties rested until the morrow, encamped within sight of each other. With sunrise, the battle was renewed, and the Saxon chief this time drove the Britons still further into the forest, but all was useless – they knew every turning and every thicket that afforded a shelter, and by the time the besiegers had again reached the town, the brave islanders were there, ready to pin the first Saxon to the wall who attempted to scale it, with the unerring javelins which they could hurl accurately to within an inch.

The forces under Ella became furious. They stood between two enemies; they were attacked both from the town and the forest; whichever way they turned, the pointed spears of the Britons were presented. At length, the Saxon chief divided his army into two bodies: one he commanded to drive the Britons into the forest, and to prevent them from returning; the other, at the same time, began to break down the walls. Revenge was now the order of the day: maddened by their losses, and irritated by the long delay, the merciless Saxons put every soul within the walls to death – neither man, woman nor child did they leave alive; such a massacre had never before taken place.

Even the walls were levelled to the earth, and, for ages after, that town stood by the gloomy forest, silent, ruined, and desolate; until even during the time of Edward the First it was pointed out to the stranger; and though the long grass and moss and lichen had grown grey upon its ruins, there were still traces of its fallen grandeur which in the words of the old chronicler, "showed how noble a city it had once been."

It is painful, even only in fancy, to picture the return of those

British warriors from the forest; how startling must have been the very silence which reigned over those ruins, the vast dreary woodland wilderness behind, the levelled walls and the bodies of the dead before – here the remains of a beloved home which the destroying fire had blackened – on the hearth a beautiful form, with her long hair steeped in her own heart's blood, her child stretched across her arm, over which the heavy rafter had in mercy fallen, the wolf already prowling about the threshold. Even through the night of time, we can almost hear their moans – each warrior reproaching himself for having fled, and envying the unbroken sleep of the slain.

How looked those British fathers and husbands when they again met the Saxon slayers in battle? Who marvels, after reading of such deeds as these, that they hung the heads of their enemies at their sides – that they found music in the gurgling of their blood – that as the foe expired they stood calmly looking on, mocking him, and telling the dying man of the wife and home he would never see again – of the savage laugh, bitter and sullen as the bursting of the sea, of the dead which in their fury they mangled – of the joy with which they hailed the flapping of the raven's wings, as they heard them descending upon the battle-field?

Thus would revenge be had, and the only marvel is, that so many beautiful passages, expressive of grief, and sorrow, and heartbroken despair, are scattered over the wild wailings of the early British bards. Yet such scenes as we have here depicted it was theirs to deplore – such revenge as they took, when the current of battle bore them on to victory, it was theirs to exult in, and their bards, gifted with the power of song, retired to mourn like the dove, or sallied forth to destruction with the scream of the eagle. They were familiar with the images of death, were called upon every day to defend their lives, and were never certain that she, whose beautiful smile beamed love on their departure in the morning, would in the evening stand waiting upon the threshold to welcome their return. Neither the weeping mother, nor the smiling child, had, in those days, power to turn aside the edge of the Saxon sword.

Thus was the second Saxon kingdom called Sussex, established by Ella, and his three sons.

Cerdric

Eighteen years later, another of Woden's descendants, named Cerdric, came with his followers in five ships. Where they landed is uncertain, though it does not appear that we should be much in error if we fixed upon Yarmouth, which for centuries after was called Cerdricksand, and known by that name even in Camden's day. At the time of his landing, the Britons were in possession of the whole island, with the exception of Kent and Sussex, and the Saxons who inhabited these kingdoms appear to have aided the new-comers. Battle followed upon battle as usual, and we are thankful that only so few scanty records exist, for it would be wearisome to go over such successive bead-rolls of slaughter.

Nor was Cerdric allowed to land peaceably, for, like Julius Cæsar five centuries before, he had to fight his way from the first moment of leaving the deck of his vessel. One great battle, however, was fought, in which the British king Natanleod was slain; the two armies met at Churdfrid, and in the onset the islanders appear to have had the advantage. Natanleod commenced the attack on the right wing of the Saxons, broke through the line, bore down the standards, and compelled Cerdric to retreat. Years had passed away since the Britons had before mustered such a force; they pursued the routed foe across the field with terrible slaughter.

The victory, however, was far from being complete, for while the Britons plunged forward, hot and eager in the pursuit, the forces under the command of the son of Cerdric closed upon the flank of the pursuing army and compelled them to wheel round and defend themselves. The Saxon chief also recovered from the panic, and attacked them in front; thus the Britons were hemmed in on both sides, and their centre was soon broken. All was now hurry, retreat, confusion, and slaughter; quarter was neither craved nor given, those who could not escape fought and fell, and when the battle was ended, the body of the British king lay surrounded by five thousand of his lifeless warriors. It will be readily imagined that Cerdric must have received great assistance from Kent and Sussex to have won such a victory, and it is evident that the leagued forces did not separate without extending their ravages – many a fair province was desolated, the inhabitants slaughtered, their houses burnt to the ground, and their priests mercilessly butchered; for wherever the Christian religion abounded, there the sword of the Saxon was found unsheathed.

*

Stuf and Wihtgar next came, both of them Cerdric's kinsmen, and it seems as if scarcely a favourable wind now blew, without wafting a fresh fleet of Saxon chiefs to the British coast. They evidently began to look upon Britain as their own; so many relations came one after the other and settled down, and never returned, that we can imagine the only topic of conversation now in Jutland was about Britain – that houses and lands were at a discount – that everybody was either purchasing or building ships – that the old crones reaped quite a harvest in standing upon the headlands and sending prayers after the vessels, for Jutes, Angles, and Saxons were now all astir; rumours had flown over the ocean that there were kingdoms for those who dare venture for them, and that, no matter how distant the descent might be, so long as the voyager had a drop of Woden's blood in his veins, there was a crown for him if he could but find followers to fight for it.

Nor had the poor Britons any hope left, for as one died off there was always another ready to succeed. Cynric followed Cerdric; he passed away, and Cealwin came – killed two or three British kings, of whom we know nothing, excepting that one was called

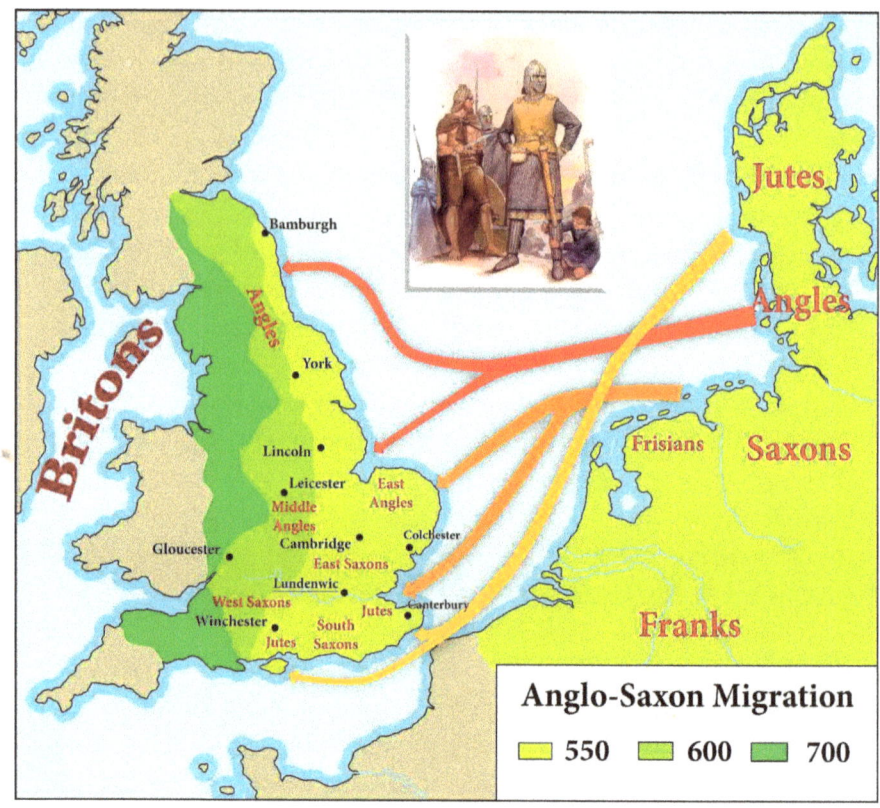

Conmail, another Condidan, and the third Farinmail – added the cities of Gloucester, Cirencester, and Bristol to his dominions – and finally established the kingdom of Wessex, which included several counties, including the Isle of Wight.

*

But we must not hurry over this stirring period, for a new champion had sprung up amongst the Britons, the king Arthur of old romance, the hero of poetry and fable, the warrior whose very existence has, to many, become a matter of doubt. What little we know of any of the British kings who existed at this period, is almost limited to the bare mention of their names.

A new language had sprung up, and, excepting among the conquered, there was no one left to record the deeds of the British heroes but the Welsh bards; for what sympathy could the

worshippers of Woden have with the warriors who spoke another language, and followed a creed so different to their own? What would we have known of the earlier Britons if it were not for Julius Cæsar? Who can doubt but that the Saxons cared only to chronicle the deeds of their own countrymen, or who can tell how many records were destroyed by the misbelieving Danes on a later day?

We have more than tradition to prove the existence of Arthur: he is alluded to by the ancient bards, and mentioned by them in succession, for as one caught up and carried forward the Cymric lay of another, so did he allude to warriors of other days. The Saxons had enough to do to record their own conquests, and left the Britons to mourn over their own disasters, for what they remembered with feelings of pride would to the new-comers be a source of regret; a British victory would but afford them a theme for a dirge, and the very memory of a hero who had occasionally triumphed over them would be a source of pain.

Those who furnished Gildas and Nennius with the subjects for their histories would not be such as kept a record of the bravery of the Britons, yet Arthur is mentioned by them both. These venerable chroniclers could but tell what they heard; many of the Welsh bards fought in the battles of which they sang, and even defeat, as well as victory, was alike woven into their lays. No such remains are found amongst the Saxon historians, yet they both mention the battles in which Arthur fought: he was a British king; and, though Gildas was living within twenty years after the death of Arthur, he had but little sympathy for him – nevertheless he praises his valour.

Arthur is the last British king in whose fortunes we can strongly sympathize. We see his native land about to be wrested from him. In every corner of the island are strangers landing, and taking possession of the soil. In almost every battle the Britons are defeated; they who, from the first dawning of history, had been the possessors of the island, are about to be driven from it, and that, too, at a period when they were just becoming familiar to us.

As we feel for and with them at this time, so do the Saxons at last interest us, and there our sympathy ends; the Normans never become so endeared to us as they have been. From their first landing we seem to dislike them, even more than we do the Saxons, whom we begin to see darkening every point of the land, for as yet they are pagans, and just as they gather upon our favour, the Danes approach; and then we feel as much interested on the side of the Saxons as we do now on that of the Britons. For there are currents in history which bear us forward against our will – we struggle against them in vain – we are swept onward through new scenes, and whirled so rapidly amongst past events, that we no longer cling to passing objects to retard our courses; but as the wide ocean opens out before us, we gaze upon its vastness in wonderment, and are lost in the contemplation of the shifting scenes which are ever chasing each other over its surface.

The forms that fall upon the pages of history are like sunshine and shadow pursuing each other over the face of the ocean, where the golden fades into the grey; and as each wave washes nearer to

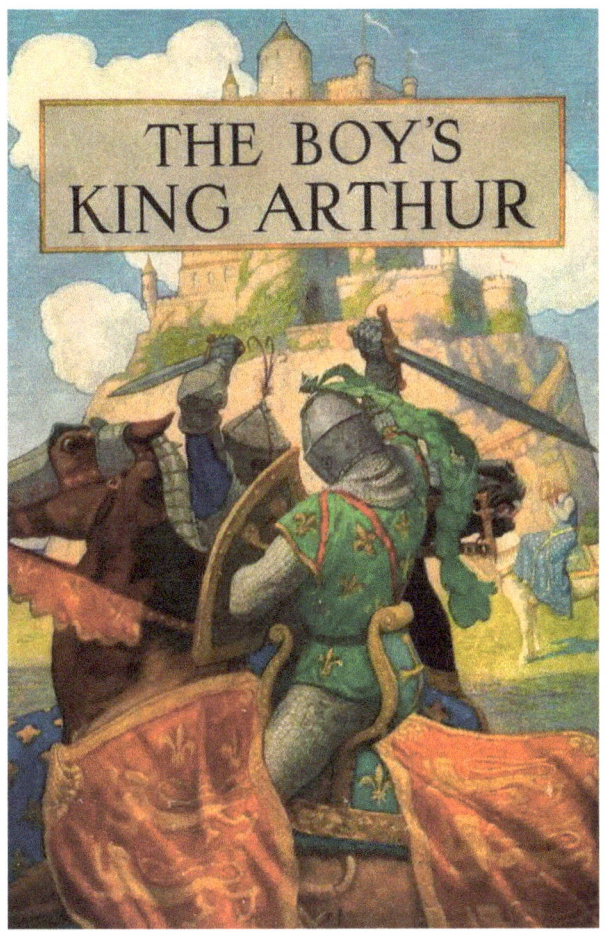

THE BOY'S KING ARTHUR

the shore, it is ever changing its hue, from gloom to brightness, until it breaks upon the beach, and is no more. Arthur leading on the Britons, with the image of the Virgin upon his shield, seems, in our eyes, only like some armed phantom, standing upon the rim of the horizon at sunset, and pointing with his sword towards the coming darkness; then he sinks behind the rounded hill, never to appear again. His twelve battles too have a glorious indistinctness – they sink one behind the other in the sunset, just as we can trace the bright armour, and the drooping banners, and the moving host, in the fading gold of the clouds – they then melt around the dying glories of heaven. Something great and grand seems ever shaping itself before the eye; but before we are able to seize upon any distinct feature, it is all gone, never to appear again.

Arthur first appears to us checking the flight of a British prince; we see his hand on the rein, he is about to bear off the beautiful lady, but is dissuaded from it by his companions. The cavalcade passes on, and he rides moodily at the head of his followers – then one of the dark turnings of time removes him from our sight.

Sword in hand, we next behold him in hot pursuit after a British chief who has slain some of his soldiers; the image of the Virgin is borne rapidly through the air, his teeth are clenched, and there is a frown upon his brow. A priest approaches – others come up – they tell him that there are enemies enough to slay amongst the Saxons. The angry spot fades from his forehead, and he sits calmly in his saddle – and again he vanishes.

His wife is then borne away, and we meet him breathing vengeance against the king of Somersetshire, vowing that he will, before night, leave Melva to sleep shorter by the head. He slackens his rein for a few moments beside the gate of a monastery: good and holy men are there, the hand of a venerable man is placed upon his bridle, the image of the Virgin he bears upon his shield is appealed to; he muses for a time with his eyes bent upon the ground, he allows his war-horse to be led under the grey gateway of the monastery – his wife is restored, and Melva forgiven, and the curtain again falls.

Huel, another king of the Britons, has been tampering with the enemies of his country; he is upbraided by Arthur for his treachery, then slain by his own hand. We see him ever in the van, at the battles of Glen, Douglas, Bassas, the Wood of Caledon, Castle Gunnion, on the banks of the Rebroit, on the mountain of Cathregonian, and the battle in which the Saxons were routed on the Badon Hills, and we no longer wonder at the slow progress made by Cerdric, or that he died before the kingdom of Wessex was established. The armed troops headed by Arthur stood in the way of his advance into Wales; they remembered the hills of Bath, and the number of slain they had left upon those summits. Saving the feud with Medrawd, in which the British king received the blow by which he died, these few facts are about all that we can gather of the renowned deeds of the mighty King Arthur.

Excepting the slight mention made of him in the works of Gildas and Nennius, the former of whom, as we have before stated, was living about the period ascribed to Arthur, we find no other record of his deeds beyond those which tradition has preserved in the words of the Welsh bards.

After the battle of Camlan, where Arthur received his death-blow, he was carried from the field, and conveyed to Glastonbury Abbey, where he was consigned to the care of a noble lady, named Morgan, who appears to have been a kinswoman of his; in her charge he was left to be cured of his wounds. He died however, though his death was long kept a secret, and rumours were sent abroad that he had been removed into another world, but would one day again appear, and reign sole king of Britain.

Ages after, it was this thought that cheered the fading eyes of the dying Celt; he believed that he left his children behind him for only a short time; and that Arthur, with the Virgin upon his shield, and his sword, 'Caliburne', in his hand, would assuredly one day come and lead the remnant of the ancient Cymry on to victory.

No historian who has looked carefully into the few facts which we possess relating to this British king has ever doubted the existence of such a belief; it was a coming devoutly looked for – the solace of a fallen nation, their only comfort when all beside had perished. It is no marvel that around his memory so many fables have been woven; that miracle upon miracle was ascribed to him, and deed upon deed piled together, until even the lofty summit of high romance at last toppled down with all its giants and monsters and improbable accumulation of enemies slain, which in the days of Gildas amounted to hundreds, and that down with it tumbled nearly all the few facts which had swelled into such an inordinate bulk from his fair fame.

How it would have astonished the true Arthur, could he but have been restored to life, and by the light of the few embers which glimmered in the British huts in the evening twilight, have heard some bard, the descendant of Llywarch the aged, who knew him well, and had looked on him, face to face, recounting his deeds at the battle of Llongberth!

Yet, through the traditions of these very bards, and by whom his deeds were so magnified, is his memory preserved, though more than thirteen centuries have passed. All belief in his return must, ages before this, have perished; yet his memory has not been forgotten, and it is on record that a secret had been entrusted to one who had probably descended from a long line of ancient minstrels; for the druids, who numbered bards amongst their order, had mysteries which they only confided to each other, and these were seldom revealed until the approach of death. Nor can we tell how much they were interested in keeping the death of Arthur a secret, for we must not forget that the fires upon their altars were not wholly extinguished when the British king fell beneath the fatal blow, which he received from the hand of his nephew in the field of Camlan, for that his death was kept a secret has never been disputed.

Though the discovery of the remains of king Arthur has long been a matter of doubt, yet while it is supported by such high authority as Giraldus Cambrensis and William of Malmsbury, who

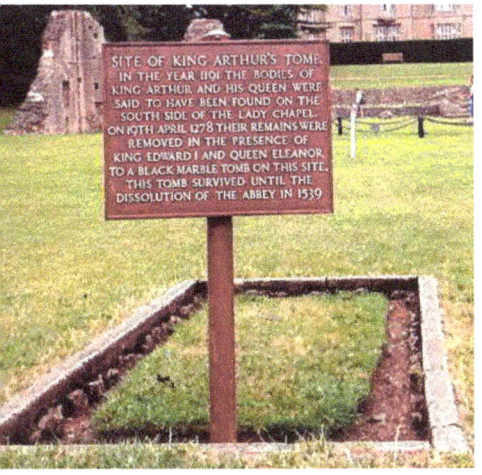

were living at the period it is said to have taken place, and while even Sharon Turner has admitted it into his *History of the Anglo-Saxons*, we should scarcely be justified in rejecting it from our pages. The discovery is said to have originated as follows.

Henry the Second, during his visits into Wales, freely admitted the Welsh bards into his presence; and as he numbered amongst his own household a minstrel of some celebrity named Pierre de Vidal, there is every reason to conclude that he was a willing listener to the ancient lays which were chanted in those days in the halls of the nobles. By one of the old British bards he was told that king Arthur was interred in Glastonbury Abbey; that the spot was marked by two pyramids, or pillars; that the body was buried very deep, to prevent the Saxons from discovering it; and that, instead of a stone coffin, the remains would be found in the trunk of a hollowed oak – a form of interment, as we have before shown, very common amongst the ancient Britons.

The king transmitted this information to the abbot of Glastonbury, commanding him to dig between the pillars, and to endeavour to discover the body of the British king. In the cemetery of the abbey, and between the monuments which the Welsh bard had pointed out, they commenced the search, and dug, it is said, until they came to a stone, under which they found a leaden cross, and the following inscription: *Hic jacet sepultus inclytus Rex Arthurus in insula Avollonia.*

Though we must confess that there is something very doubtful about the inscription of a British king not being in Welsh, when the Cymry were said, at this period, to have been acquainted with letters, we will pass it by, and go on with the narrative.

Sixteen feet lower, it is said, they found the outer coffin, which, as before described, was formed out of the solid stem of an oak, hollowed in the centre to contain the body. The leg-bones, we are told, were of an unusual size, being the breadth of three fingers longer than those of the tallest man present. These bones Giraldus took in his hand and also read the inscription, for he was present at the disinterment. The skull was large, and marked with ten wounds – nine of these had healed in the bone, the tenth was open, and probably showed where the mortal blow was struck. Near at hand were found the remains of his wife; the long yellow hair which the ancient bards loved to dwell upon in their descriptions of the fair queen appeared perfect, until touched.

The remains were removed into the abbey, and placed in a magnificent shrine, which, by the order of Edward the First, was placed before the high altar. In the year 1276, nearly a hundred years after the bodies were discovered, the same king, accompanied by his queen, visited Glastonbury, and had the shrine opened to look upon the remains of the renowned warrior and his once fair consort. King Edward folded the bones of the reputed Arthur in a rich shroud, while his wife did the same with those of the yellow-haired queen; then placed them again reverentially within the shrine. The pillars which marked the spot where the bodies were discovered long remained; and William of Malmsbury, who was living at the period when they were disinterred, has left an account of the inscription and figures upon the pillars, which were five-sided, and twenty-six feet high.

Neither the meanings of the inscriptions, or the figures, were at the period of their discovery rightly understood. What befel them afterwards we know not, though the fate of the abbey is well known. Whether the discovery of these remains be true or not, there cannot be a doubt about the existence of king Arthur; for, were there even no allusion made to him by Gildas and Nennius, who lived near upon the period when he was waging war with Cerdric and Cealwin; or by the British bards, who knew him personally, and even fought under his command – were there no such undeniable evidence as the above, the traditions which so long preserved his remembrance would go far to prove his existence.

But these throw no light upon the achievements by which he

the tube of kyng Arthour

became so renowned; it is like discovering the casket without the gem – there is evidence of the treasure, and also of the care with which it was preserved, but what the treasure itself was, we know not. What few facts we have thrown together are all that can really be depended upon as the true history of king Arthur: his knights, his round table, and the deeds which are attributed to him, must ever stand amongst the thousand-and-one tales which a wonder-loving people have treasured in all ages, and some of which are found even amongst the most barbarous nations.

They appear to have been such as raised Woden into a god in the darkest era of Saxon paganism; and as Roman civilization seems never to have spread far amongst the ancient Cymry in Wales, we are justified in concluding that they also loved to cast around the memory of their bravest chieftain the same mysterious reverence, and that what was needed to make up the unnatural stature of the image of their idolatry, they piled up from old legends and fables, that 'give delight, but hurt not.'

The matter of Arthur's remains, then, is doubtful history.

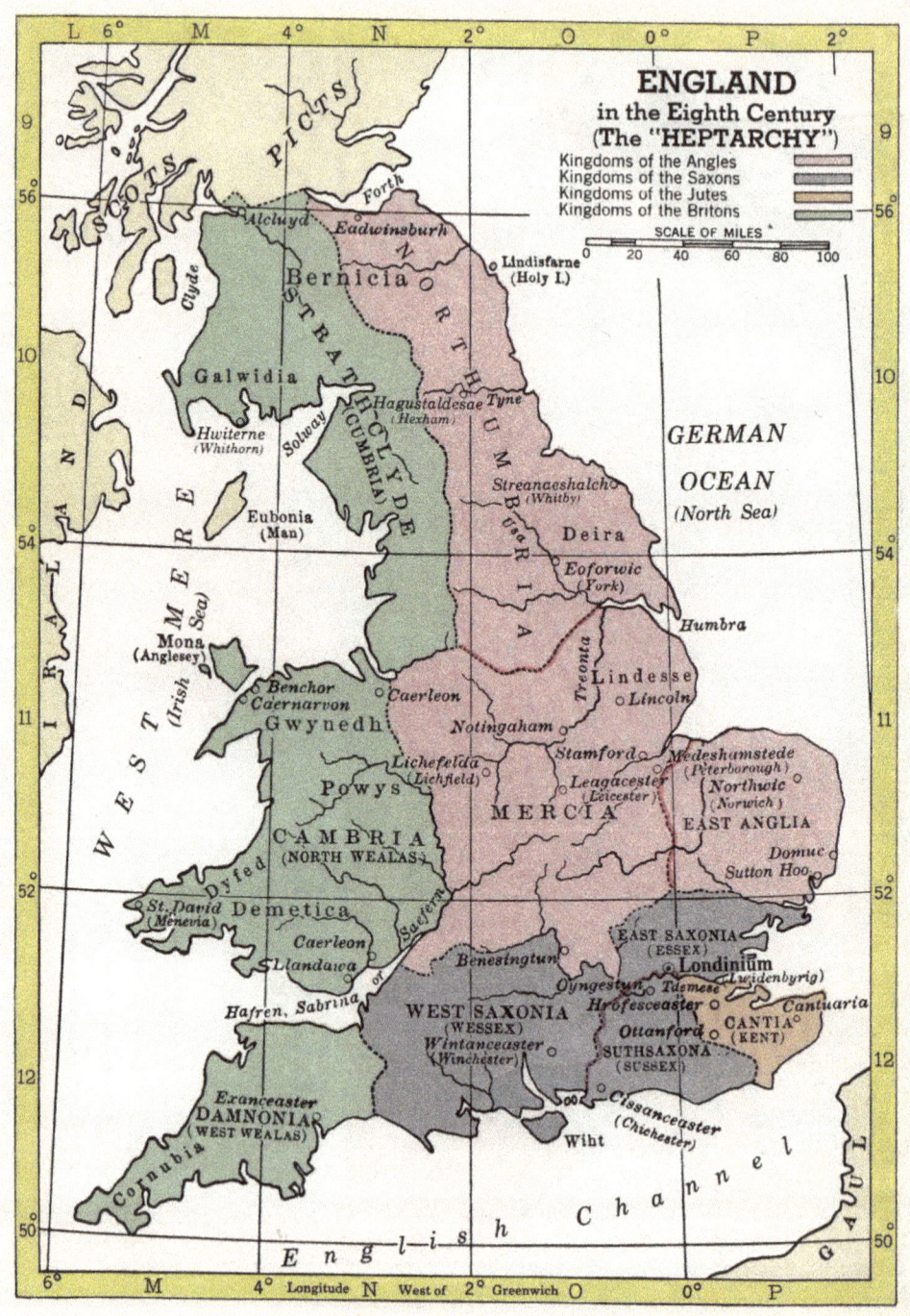

11 THE ESTABLISHMENT OF THE SAXON OCTARCHY

Over the hawk's station, over the hawk's banquet of heads,
Over the quivering of the spears, reddening was the wing;
Over the howling of the storm
the course of the sea-gull was seen;
Over the blood, whirling and flowing,
the exulting ravens were screaming,
They hovered above the treasure of the fierce-winged race,
And their clamour went spreading through the sky.

– Cynddelu's *Death of Owen*

During the period in which the events occurred that are narrated in the opening pages of our last chapter, another body of Saxons had arrived in Britain, and settled down in Essex, where under Erkenwin they laid the foundation of that kingdom or state which eventually extended into Middlesex, and included London – then a town of considerable note, though bearing no marks of its high destiny, as its few houses heaved up and overlooked the Thames.

Little did the fisherman dream, as he turned back to gaze upon his humble home where the morning sunbeams fell, that the hut in which he had left his children asleep stood where a city would one day rise – a city which would become the metropolis of England, and the envy of surrounding nations. Still less did those ancient Saxons, as they landed in the marshes of Essex, ever imagine that they were marching onward towards a town whose renown would one day spread to the uttermost ends of the earth, a city which would at last arrest the gaze of the whole wide world, whose grandeur would only be eclipsed by its greatness, and stand as the sun of the earth, defying all eyes to point out, amid the blaze of its splendour, where its brightness began or where it ended.

But while the tide which bore on a new population was thus setting in, and the kingdom of East Anglia was formed by a portion of the Saxon tribe who have left no other names behind than those given to the counties of Suffolk and Norfolk, the most formidable force that had hitherto arrived in Britain since the time of the Romans landed between the Tweed and the Firth of Forth. Forty ships anchored near the mouths of these rivers, and from them stepped onto shore Ida and his twelve sons, with a number of nameless chiefs, who belonged to the tribe of Angles, and a long train of Saxon followers, all of whom had sworn to acknowledge Ida as their king, for he also claimed descent from the inexhaustible stock of Woden.

Between the Clyde and the Humber, the country was divided amongst many of the British tribes, all of whom had their separate king, or chief, and who were always doing their utmost, unconsciously, to aid the conquest of the Saxons, by waging war with each other. Bernicia and Deira, as they were afterwards called, were at the time of Ida's landing governed by the following kings or chiefs, for it is difficult to distinguish their proper titles: they were named Gall, Dyvedel, Ysgwnell, Urien, the patron of Taliesin the bard, Rhydderc the generous, Gwallog, and Aneurin, himself a poet – together with other sovereigns whose very names have perished, and who all appear to have, for once, united and made a bold stand against the advance of Ida.

We have now the light of these ancient bards to guide us

through this remote period, and some of them fought in the very battles of which they have left us descriptions. Chief amongst these British warriors appears to have been Urien; Taliesin calls him the "shield of heroes, the thunderbolt of the Cymry," and compares his onset to "the rushing of mighty waves, and fiery meteors blazing athwart the heavens." Ida, they designated the flame-man, or flame-bearer, so terrible was the devastation which he made.

Many battles were fought between these renowned chieftains. It was on the night which ushers in the Sabbath when the 'flame-bearer' approached, with his forces divided into four companies, to surround Goddeu and Reged, provinces over which Urien governed. Ida spread out his forces from Argoedd to Arfynnydd, and having assumed this threatening position, he daringly demanded submission and hostages from the Britons. Urien indignantly spurned the proposition, and turning to his brother chieftains, exclaimed:

> "Let us raise our banners where the mountain winds blow – let us dash onward with our forces over the border – let each warrior lift his spear above his head, and rush upon the destroyer, in the midst of his army, and slay him, together with his followers."

Taliesin, who was present and fought under the banner of Urien, thus describes the 'Battle of the Pleasant Valley':

> "When the shouts of the Britons ascended, louder than the roaring of the waves upon the storm-tossed shore, neither field nor forest afforded safety to the foe: I saw the warriors in their brave array, I saw them after the morning's strife – oh, how altered! I saw the conflict between the perishing hosts, the blood that gushed forward and soaked into the red ground: – the valley which was defended by a rampart was no longer green. Wan, weary men, pale with affright, and stained with blood, dropped their arms and staggered across the ford; I saw Urien, with his red brow – his sword fell on the bucklers of his enemies with deadly force – he rushed upon them like an eagle enraged."

In this battle, the Britons appear to have been victorious – others followed in which they were defeated, for the 'flame-bearing man' spread terror wherever he trod. He, however, at last fell by Owen the son of Urien, one of the poets, who also perished by the hand of one of his own countrymen, and his death was bemoaned by the British bard Llywarch, in such a plaintive strain that there are few compositions which excel this ancient elegy, for its beautiful pathos and wild, mournful images:

> "I bear a head from the mountains; the body will before night be buried under the cairn of stones and earth! Where is he that supported and feasted me? Euryddiel will be joyless to-night. Whom shall I praise, now Urien is no more? The hall is stricken into ruins, the floor desolate, where many a hound and hawk were trained for the chase. Nettles and weeds will grow over that hearth, which, when Urien lived, was ever open to the tread of the needy; the shout of the warriors as they uplifted the mead cups, no more will be heard rioting. The decaying green will cover it, the mouldering lichen will conceal it, the thorn will above it grow; the cauldron will become rusted that seethed the

deer, the sword of the warrior will no longer clank over it, no sound of harmony will again be heard there; where once the blazing torches flashed, and the deep drinking horn went round, the swine will root and the black ants swarm, for Urien is no more!"

Such were the immortal echoes that floated around our island, nearly a thousand years before Shakespeare 'struck the golden lyre'.

After the death of Urien, another severe battle was fought in the north between the Britons and the Angles, who had accompanied Ida. Aneurin, who was in the fight, has composed the longest poem which has descended to us describing these ancient conflicts; it is called the *Gododin*, and was held in such reverence by the Welsh bards that they called him their king. It is frequently alluded to by the minstrels of the period. The poem is descriptive of the battle of Cattraeth, from which Aneurin escaped, when three hundred and three score British nobles, all wearing the 'golden torque', fell. It contains nearly a thousand lines.

Only three renowned warriors survived this awful combat; the bard was amongst the number. The British chieftains had been drinking pale mead by 'the light of rushes' all night long; with the first streak of dawn, they set out to attack the Saxons; when they came in sight of the enemy, they "hastened swift, all running together – and short were their lives".

Like a melancholy chorus in a dirge, this 'pale mead' banquet is repeatedly mentioned throughout the poem; its effects are sadly deplored, it is ever turning up and coming in upon the end of some sorrowful reflection;

> "pleasant was its taste, long its woe – it had been their feast, and was their poison – it was a banquet for which they paid the price of their lives."

Hear Aneurin's own words:

> "The warriors that went to Cattraeth were furious – pale golden wine and mead had they drank; they were three hundred and three score and three, all wearing golden torques, who hastened to battle after the banquet. From the edges of the keen-slaying swords, only three escaped the war-dogs. Aeron and Dayarawd and I, from the flowing blood were saved. The reward of my protecting muse."

The battle appears to have been fought in the morning of one of their festive days; and in the grey dawn, the intoxicated chiefs ran upon the enemy all together, probably having boasted over their cups that one would outstrip the other, and be the first to dye his sword in Saxon blood. The scene of the battle cannot now be ascertained; that it was in the north we have proof, from the men of Bernicia and Deiri being present.

After these events, the kingdom called Mercia was established; it appears to have extended over our present midland counties, occupying the most important space which stretches from the Severn to the Humber, and even pushing its frontier upon the borders of Wales. This formed the eighth kingdom, state, or colony, established by the Saxons since the day when Hengist and Horsa first entered the service of Vortigern – a period occupying but little more than one hundred years, and during that time there was scarcely an interval in which the Saxons had not either to defend their hard-won possessions, or aid their countrymen when they were close pressed.

The Britons had still their own kingdoms in Wales, Cornwall, a portion of Devonshire, and the district of Strathclyde; and some of these they maintained even after the death of Alfred.

We will now take a rapid glance at the eight kingdoms established by the Saxons, for although Bernicia and Deiri are frequently classed to-gether as one state, and called Northumbria, and were occasionally under the sway of one sovereign, they were, nevertheless, distinct kingdoms for a time. Thus an octarchy was established, formed of the following eight distinct states.

First, the Jutes, who had gained Kent, where Hengist first established himself, and to which his followers added the Isle of Wight, and a portion of the opposite coast of Hampshire. This formed the kingdom of **Kent**.

Second, the South Saxons, who landed under Ella, and, after severe combat with the Britons, founded the kingdom of **Sussex**.

Third, the East Saxons, who, under the command of Erkenwin, gradually spread over the counties of Essex, Middlesex, and the southern portion of Hertfordshire, which afterwards became known as the kingdom of **Essex**.

THE ANGLO-SAXON KINGDOMS, CA. 800

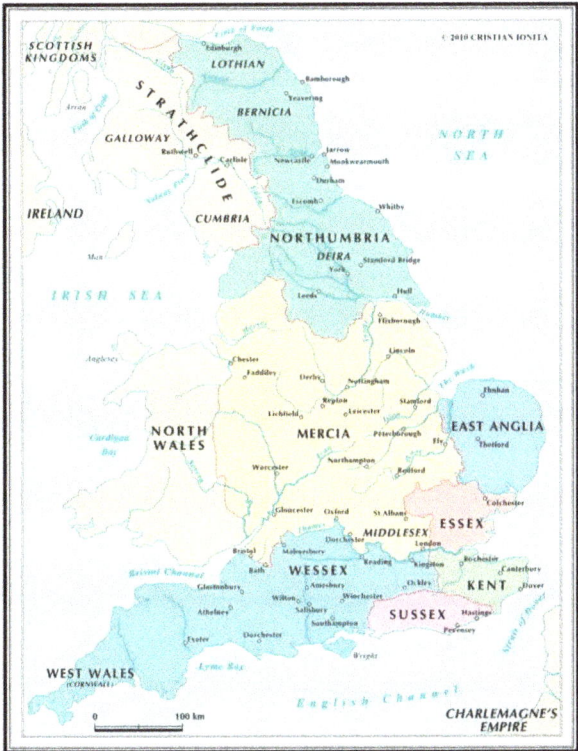

Fourth, the West Saxons, who, headed by Cerdric, conquered the inhabitants of Surrey, part of Hampshire, Berkshire, Wiltshire, Dorsetshire, Somerset, a portion of Devonshire and Cornwall (though long after this period), and finally, founded the kingdom of **Wessex**.

Fifth, East Anglia, containing Norfolk, Suffolk, Cambridge, the Isle of Ely, and some portion of Bedfordshire, all included in the state or kingdom of **East Anglia**.

Sixth, **Deiri**, which included the counties of Lancaster, York, Westmoreland, Cumberland, and Durham.

Seventh, **Bernicia**, where Ida first landed, and which extended from Northumberland into Scotland, somewhere between the rivers Forth and Tweed.

Eighth, and last, **Mercia**, which swallowed up the chief portion of the midland counties, and was divided into the north and south by the river Trent, though all were within the limits of the dominion of Mercia.

Such were the kingdoms that formed the Saxon Octarchy, and which were no sooner established, than one state began to wage war against the other, in which they were occasionally aided by various Britons.

Hitherto we have had to feel our way cautiously along the shores which skirt the dark sea of History, and have been compelled to put into many a creek and harbour at a venture, as abler mariners have done before us; but, in no instance have we stirred without consulting the compass and carefully examining the chart which Gildas, Nennius, and Bede, those ancient voyagers, have drawn up as a guide – and which Turner and MacCabe 1 have carefully examined, and marked anew every point that is dark and doubtful.

Many events transpired before the final establishment of the Saxon Octarchy, which we have hurriedly passed over as being of little importance, and which to have narrated would have carried us again over the ground already traversed. Of such are the deaths of the various Saxon kings or chiefs; the contests that arose in selecting a successor, and the bickerings and breakings out, which were necessarily consequent upon the formation of so many separate states; for few of them could be called kingdoms.

Nor must we suppose that in all cases where the conquerors settled down, the British inhabitants fled before them. Many doubtless remained behind, and gradually intermixed with the Saxons; including those who had grown civilized under the Roman government, and were skilled in the arts and manufactures, and had still continued to improve in agriculture, ever since the time of Agricola. Men possessing this knowledge, and acquainted with these secrets, would be tempted to reside amongst the invaders; and so we shall soon arrive at a period which will show that civilization had tamed down the martial spirit of the Saxon, as it had already done that of the Britons, with the result that they were for a long time as apparently helpless under the attacks of the Danes as had been the ancient inhabitants of the island under their own repeated assaults.

It would be a work of great labour, and one that would require an acute analysis, to trace, step by step, this degenerative process.

Many of the Britons emigrated. We have shown that twelve thousand, under a free king, Riothamus, went out to war against the Visigoths, but it would only be carrying us into the history of other countries were we to follow their footsteps. Even the Britons that remained behind, though dispossessed of nearly the whole of their country for a long time, 'bated not a jot of heart nor hope'. They clung to their old prophecies, and, through the dark night of oppression, believed that they would before long break into the bright morning of vengeance, when they would drive the Saxons before them triumphantly out of Britain.

Strengthened by this belief, they fought many a battle which we have not recorded, and even when defeated, it was only to retire to their 'stony paradise,' as their bards called Wales, and there await the breaking of that bright morning which had so long been foretold. There is something wild and beautiful in the very idea of this never-to-be-realised hope; it forms a prominent feature in the character of the Welsh population to this very day, though now turned into a feeling, which arms them, better than any other, against the lesser evils of life. They are ever in the hope of seeing 'better days'.

*

We can readily imagine that every rumour of warfare amongst the Saxon tribes, must have been received with as much acclaim in their mountain fortresses, as would the first note awakened by Aneurin or Llywarch when they struck their harps.

We can picture the eagerness with which they hurried down, to aid one Saxon chief to make war upon another, scarcely caring which chief conquered, so long as they themselves escaped, and believing that the body of every enemy which they left in the field was a step closer to the fulfilment of their own freedom.

They never lacked a leader if an attack was contemplated, and we probably err not in surmising that many an onset was made after the night had been consumed 'by the light of the rushes,' and while they were brimful of valour and 'pale mead', and heated by the lay which some bard less renowned than Aneurin chanted.

Cattraeth may not be the only instance in which the wearers of the golden torques, the ensign of British nobility, fell. Still there seems to have been a hearty faith in the ancient Cymry, which endears them to us, and in nothing was this evinced more than in their belief of the predictions of their bards. A pale ray of light, like the lingering of a subdued smile, falls upon our page whilst we write, as we contrast 'then' with 'now'.

The bards of other days were kings, chiefs, and renowned warriors; their harps raised them to these dignities. The bards of the present day are bards only, and however great their fame, can only receive due honour by first passing through the gate of death. The extracts with which we have enriched this chapter show the appreciation of the beautiful, in a barbarous age, and let not this sentence be forgotten. All that we know of the lives of many of those ancient British kings, who were great and renowned in their day, is what has been preserved in the lays of our early bards; but for these, their very names would have perished, and Urien himself would never again have awakened the throb of a human heart.

The cold contempt of the proud and the haughty chilled not the heart of the true minstrel. With his harp in his heart he ever goes, making music his companion, when there is none beside to hear it; and the notes he often carelessly scatters behind him, if of the true tone, are never lost. A thousand years pass away, and they still ring as freshly in the heart as those which we have here gathered, and which Llywarch, more than 1,300 years ago, poured forth between his sighs when he mourned for the loss of his chieftain. There is a sadness about the dirges which we still feel.

The monuments of brass, iron and marble have ages ago decayed or mouldered away, yet the echoes which arose from that ancient harp have not yet died. Time destroys all things, except the immortality of the human mind.

12 THE CONVERSION OF ETHELBERT

> The oracles are dumb, no voice or hideous hum
> Runs through the archëd roof, in words deceiving.
> Apollo from his shrine can no more divine,
> With hollow shriek the steep of Delphos leaving.
> No nightly trance or breathéd spell
> Inspires the pale-eyed priest from the prophetic cell.
>
> – Milton

Many of the early Saxon chieftains, or kings, for it matters not by which title we call them, had by this time died, and been succeeded by their sons and kinsmen. That many had also perished in the wars with the Britons we have already shown, and now when the Octarchy was established, and the ancient inhabitants of the country were either conquered or driven into one corner of the island – when it might be expected that Peace had at last alighted and taken up her abode in the land – the Saxon sovereigns began to war with each other.

We have before shown that when the Saxons went out to battle, they selected a king. No matter how high might be the rank of those who had sworn to serve under him, they obeyed his commands; when the war was over, each again stepped into his former dignity, and the power thus given for a time to the war-king was at an end.

Some such king was acknowledged by the Saxon sovereigns, and he was called the *bretwalda*, or king of Britain, though it is not clear that the other sovereigns ever paid him any homage, and the only inference we can draw from the claim set up by Ethelbert, the young king of Kent, is that it was conferred upon that prince who was the nearest kin to Woden.

Something of the kind is shadowed forth in the claim, which is grounded alone on his descent from Hengist. Ella, king of Sussex, appears to have been the first to bear the title of *bretwalda* in Britain; he died, and it seems as if some time elapsed before any other of the Saxon kings assumed the title.

The next that did was Ceawlin, king of Wessex. Ethelbert of Kent rose up, and disputed the claim. Ceawlin was not a man to be moved from his high estate by the descendant of Hengist, and from this dispute sprang the first civil war between the Saxon kings.

Ethelbert was but little more than sixteen, when he so daringly threw defiance in the face of the king of Wessex, and Ceawlin was at that time one of the most powerful of all the Saxon kings. After having defeated Ethelbert, on the death of Cissa, king of Sussex, he annexed that kingdom to his own; nor was there a sovereign throughout the whole Saxon states bold enough to wrest the plunder from his hand.

For a youth like Ethelbert to have thus bearded so powerful a king, and to have been the first to commence hostilities, and finally to have succeeded in gaining the envied title, evinces a courage and a perseverance which draw the eye anxiously forward to watch the result of his future career, nor shall we be disappointed in the issue. But, before passing to the most important event in his life, we must detail the circumstances by which it was brought on.

*

One day, as a monk named Gregory was passing through the market of Rome, gazing upon the great variety of treasures which were piled there, and for which nearly every corner of Europe had been ransacked, he was struck by a group of beautiful boys. There was something in their white limbs, fair complexions, and light long flowing hair, which at once arrested the eye of the kind-hearted monk.

He turned to a keen-eyed merchant who was awaiting a purchaser (and who had probably other things beside these boys to sell), and inquired from what country they had been brought.

Britain, was the answer.

The next question he asked was whether the inhabitants were Christians or Pagans? He was told that they were Pagans.

Gregory sighed heavily when he heard this, and, as he fixed his eye with a tender and pitiful look upon these fair and beautiful slaves, he exclaimed:

"Oh, grief of griefs! that the author of darkness should lay claim to beings of such fair forms – that there should be so much grace in the countenance, yet none in the soul."

When told that they were of the race of the Angles, he said they were worthily named, for their faces were angelic; and when informed that the province from which they came was called the Deiri, he paused, divided the word, dwelt upon it, then exclaimed,

"*De-ira Dei* (from the wrath of God) they must be torn."

But when he further heard that the king of the country from whence they came was named Ella, the beautiful picture which had opened before his imagination, merely conjured up from the ideas created by suggestive sound, was complete, and, in his happy enthusiasm, he exclaimed,

"Hallelujah! The praise of God must be sung in that land."

Imagine the quivering lip and tearful eye which would first show the impression of a kind-hearted man and a scholar, when told that these fair children had been dragged from their homes, and brought from a distant island, far away over the sea, and stood there huddled together, seeking to avoid the merciless eye of the unfeeling merchant, who found them the most troublesome part of the cargo he had brought, for the bales he probably sat upon required no feeding, and as a point of business, he had been compelled to keep those young slaves plump and in good order, and doubtless, while showing them to the monk, he made them display themselves to the best advantage.

They, struck by the kindness which must have beamed, like a glory, around the countenance of the good monk Gregory, perhaps wished that they might be purchased by so friendly-looking a master, for they would be unable to comprehend a single word he said, beyond the names of their country and kings.

The quivering lip and tearful eye would soon change into the lighted look of enthusiasm, as, bit by bit, the pagan island rose before the fancy of the tender-hearted monk, as he saw their beautiful heathen mothers and fair sisters kneeling before senseless stocks and stones; and oh! what a chill must have come over his kind heart when the pope, whom he entreated to send missionaries into that heathen land, rejected his petition.

Still, it did not deter Gregory from purchasing the slaves who had so deeply interested him. He further clothed and educated them, and would, had he not been prevented, have accompanied them on their return to Britain.

Monk Gregory at last became the Roman pontiff; but the splendour by which he was now surrounded altered not his gentle nature, and he remembered those beautiful barbarians.

He had many a time thought of their island home over the waves, and the fair mothers who looked in vain for their return. He solicited a monk – to whom he had doubtless before-time confided this wish, which ever seems to have been nearest his heart – to undertake the journey; and Augustine was chosen to fulfil this mission.

The monks who were appointed to attend Augustine in his mission had heard such rumours of the ferocity of the Saxons that they expressed a desire to return to Rome, although they had proceeded some distance on their journey. They so far gave way to their fears as to prevail upon Augustine to go back and solicit the pope to recall them.

The pontiff, however, told them that to abandon an undertaking which they had commenced was more disgraceful than if they had not accepted it; he bade them proceed in God's name, he appointed Augustine abbot over them, and commanded them to obey him. Further, he gave them letters to the prelates and kings through whose countries they would have to pass.

To the daughter of Charibert, king of the Franks, Ethelbert was married; and although she was a Christian, and he a pagan, it had been no bar to their union; Bertha was to follow her own creed, Ethelbert his: he bowed before Woden, she acknowledged the existence of the true God. Vortigern and Rowena had lived together on the same terms before-time.

Augustine arrived in Britain, with his train of fifty monks and interpreters which the king of the Franks had provided, and landed in the isle of Thanet.

How different the intent of his mission to that of the Saxon chiefs who had landed there a century and a half before him! They had come to kill, to earn their wages by bloodshed; these came to save, and were neither armed with spear, sword, nor axe; their only shield was the cross of Christ, and on their banner the figure of the Redeemer was borne. They came with no other war-cry than the Litany which they chanted as they moved gravely along.

What glorious scenes illustrative of the progress of our religion yet remain to be painted!

How easy to picture that ancient procession as it passed: their landing from the ship: their prayer offered up on the beach: the misbelieving Saxons looking on in wonder: some priest of Woden pouring into the ear of a listening chief a disparaging story: the countenances of children looking on with a mixture of fear and wonder: heathen mothers pitying the figure upon the banner, and wondering what he had done to be nailed upon the cross.

Or perhaps thinking that they had come to solicit aid against those who had been guilty of such inhuman cruelty, and their motherly hearts at once enlisted in favour of the strangers, who came to seek the means of vengeance for such an outrage.

Or perhaps they pitied the poor monks who had no arms to defend themselves, and entreated their husbands to assist them.

Such fancies would naturally float over their benighted minds, for at what other conclusions could they arrive from what they now saw? Doubtless the ship, when first seen out at sea, would awaken other thoughts, and many an armed figure paced the shore impatiently, and awaited the arrival of the vessel, drawing circles upon the sand with their pointed weapons, to while away the time, as they stood ready to offer up fresh victims on the altar of Odin.

Ethelbert received the tidings of their coming rather coldly, but still not unkindly; he bade them to remain where they were, supplied them with such things as their immediate wants required, and promised, in the meantime, to consider what he would do for them.

The bright eyes of Bertha had exerted their influence; her sweet voice had made an inroad into the stony heart of Ethelbert; but for her beautiful face, he would probably have consigned the whole race of trembling monks to Neiflheim and Hela the terrible, or offered them up as a rich sacrifice to Odin.

But even Bertha, great as her power appears to have been over him, could only influence him in their favour by slow degrees; he deliberated for several days before he consented to meet them, and when he did at last agree to a conference, he chose the open air – still true to his ancient faith, for there he had been taught to believe that all magical influence was powerless.

How looked he when he first beheld them? Perhaps he clung to the fair Christian that stood by his side, and as she pressed his arm, and he felt that she also was of the same faith, the colour mounted his cheek for a moment, and, as it would appear, his heart half reproached him for having treated them so coldly, for he at once kindly commanded the missionaries to sit down. Doubtless the spot chosen for this interview was a circle surrounded with seats of turf, such as the Saxons assembled in, in the early ages, when their *witenagemots* (assemblies) were held in the open air.

Surrounded with his nobles, the king listened attentively while Augustine made known the object of his mission. Ethelbert, who was endowed with clear judgment, waited patiently till the abbot had finished, and then answered:

> "Your promises are fair, but new and uncertain. I cannot abandon the rites which my people have hitherto observed; but as you have come a long way to tell us what you believe to be true, we will not only hold you harmless, but treat you hospitably. Nor will we forbid any one you can convince to join in your faith."

Such was the substance of Ethelbert's answer; a more candid or a kinder one never issued from a pagan's lips; but those lips had been breathed on by the prayers of Bertha, and her own rounded roses had kissed their way into his heart. He had found the honey that hung upon them to be far sweeter than the richest sacrifice that ever steamed up from the altars of Woden.

Ethelbert gave them a church in Canterbury, which was built in the time of the Romans.

The British Christians had there bowed to their Maker; it had been Bertha's place of worship, and was probably the only one in the wide county of Kent where prayers to the true God were offered up – where she herself had many a time, amid hopes and fears, prayed for the day to come which had at last arrived. She, a stranger in a foreign land, far away from the home of her fathers, surrounded by pagan altars and the hideous images of rude idols, had never once despaired, as she leant, like Hope, upon her anchor, with no one near to comfort her, but even while the hymns of Odin rang upon her ear, in the midst of her devotions, had kept her eye fixed upon the star which was mirrored in the troubled waters that washed around the cold anchor, and chilled her naked feet.

In this ancient British church, Augustine and his monks administered the rites and ceremonies of the Christian religion unmolested. Numerous converts were soon made and baptised, and chief amongst these was king Ethelbert himself.

As a proof of his earnestness and sincerity, the newly converted Saxon sovereign granted the monks permission to repair all the British churches in his kingdom, which had before-time been devoted to Christian worship. The pope also conferred on Augustine the title of archbishop, and sent him over a pall, woven from the purest and whitest lambs wool, and chequered with purple crosses, that, when worn over his shoulders, it might remind him of Christ the good Shepherd, and of the crosses and perils he endured in bringing home the lost sheep on his shoulders, and gathering them together in the fold.

But vestments for the altar, sacerdotal garments, sacred vessels and relics of martyrs were not all that Gregory sent over to Britain; for manuscript Bibles, copies of the Gospels, psalters, and legends of the saints and martyrs were among the more substantial treasures which the learned pope poured into our island, and some of which our own immortal Alfred translated with his own hand in a later day.

The bindings of many of these manuscripts were emblazoned with silver images of our Saviour, and glittering glories of yellow gold, from the centre of which blazed precious stones, so that when uplifted by the priest, who stood high above their heads as he expounded the holy mysteries, their eyes were dazzled by the splendour of those richly bound volumes, and their senses impressed with a solemn reverence, as they looked upon the image of their Redeemer.

He also sent over other fellow-labourers, and amongst these were men distinguished for their piety and learning. Gregory was a man endowed with great discernment, possessing also those peculiar qualities which have ever marked the profoundest statesmen; in these essentials he stood high above his archbishop Augustine.

The far-seeing pope knew that he had to deal with a race of idolaters, many of whom would change their creed to please their sovereign, or from other interested motives; and, conscious of the purity of his own design and the holiness of his cause, he resolved that there should be nothing startling or forbidding, or much at variance with their ancient customs, in the outward signs and ceremonies of the Christian religion. With a liberality of opinion far outstriding that of the age, he rightly concluded, that whatever was not really evil in itself, it was useless to abolish.

Let them retain their sacrifices, argued Gregory; when the idols are removed, and the remembrance of them destroyed, let them slaughter their cattle, sacrifice, and feast upon the offering, and thank God for his great abundance. What mattered it if on saint-days they erected arbours of green branches around the church, feasted, and made merry within them, so long as it was done in remembrance of the saint to whom the building was dedicated?

Surely this was better than holding such celebration in honour of senseless idols. Even their pagan temples he would not allow to be hurled down, conscious that if such places had been held sacred while set apart for the worship of graven images of wood or stone, they would be doubly revered when the light of the true gospel broke in glory within those ancient walls.

Pope Gregory had, doubtless, become acquainted with the principal points of their heathen faith, and had concluded that if only rapine and slaughter, and brave but brutal deeds, had been extolled within those walls, and were the sure passports that opened the envied halls of Valhalla, he might safely venture to wrestle with this pagan idol, and overthrow him upon his own ground. And further, that the doctrines which breathed only of peace and goodwill, and love and charity, and holy faith in a dying Redeemer, would still be the same if offered up from the very altars on which Odin himself had stood.

It was the substance and the spirit which dawned upon the great intellectual eye of Pope Gregory, and made him tread boldly amongst the broken idols which lay scattered at his feet, where others would have hesitated to have moved. He daringly grafted the true faith upon a heathen stock, well knowing that neither the stem nor the soil would militate against the growth of the goodly fruit with which the branches would on a future day be hung.

Gregory would never have entered into that fatal controversy beneath the oak, as Augustine had done, about the celebration of Easter Sunday, and which, if it did not lead to the slaughter of the monks of Bangor, as some have believed, lessened the archbishop in the eyes of the English priests, and caused much dissension and bitter feeling amongst the Saxons.

But Ethelbert, Bertha, and Augustine died; and Eadbald

became king of Kent.

Eadbald took possession of his father's throne and widow at the same time; for, after the death of Bertha, Ethelbert had married another princess of the same nation as his former wife. The priests raised their voices and denounced the marriage of Eadbald with his step-mother; he heeded them not, but turned pagan again, and a great portion of his subjects changed their religion with him.

Sigebert, the king of Essex, his father's friend, who had become a Christian, also died about this time, and his sons again embraced their old heathen creed, though they still occasionally visited the Christian church.

They were one day present while the bishop was administering the Eucharist. They asked:

> "Why dost thou not offer us that white bread which thou art giving to others, and which thou wert wont to give to our father's sib?"

The bishop replied that if they would wash in the same font in which their father the king was baptized when he became a Christian, they might partake of the white bread.

They replied that they would not be washed in the fountain, yet they still demanded the bread. The bishop refused to give it them, and the heathen chiefs drove the monks out of Essex. Some of them went into Kent, others left Britain for a time; and as the remnant were on the eve of departing, Eadbald, by a strange interposition, again renounced his pagan faith, and intreated the priests to remain behind, promising also to assist them, as his father Ethelbert had before done, in the work of conversion.

Whether it was a dream, or the reproaches of his own conscience, or the penance which Laurence had inflicted upon himself, before he again appeared in the presence of Eadbald – or even the working of His mighty hand "who moves in a mysterious way his wonders to perform" – can never be known. Suffice it to say that the Saxon king saw the error of his ways, and repented.

13 EDWIN, KING OF THE DEIRI AND BERNICIA

> How oft do they their silver bowers leave
> To come to succour us that succour want;
> How oft do they with golden pinions cleave
> The flitting skies, like flying pursuivant,
> Against foul fiends to aid us militant;
> They for us fight, they watch, and duly ward,
> And their bright squadrons round about us plant,
> And all for love, and nothing for reward;
> Oh! Why should heavenly God to men have such regard?
>
> – Spenser's *Faery Queen*

Bernicia and the Deiri formed, at this period, two Saxon kingdoms which lay bordering each other. Ethelfrith governed the portion that stretched from Northumberland to between the Tweed and the Frith of Forth; and Ella, dying, left his son Edwin, then an infant, to succeed him as king of the Deiri – a part of England now divided into the counties of Lancaster, York, Westmoreland, Cumberland, and Durham.

The Northumbrian king, Ethelfrith, appears at this time to have been the most powerful of all the Saxon monarchs; and no sooner was Ella dead, than he took possession of the Deiri; nor was a sovereign to be found throughout the whole of the Saxon kingdoms bold enough to draw his sword in defence of Edwin. The child was, however, carried into Wales, and entrusted to the care of Cadvan, who was himself a British king, though now driven into the very corner of those territories over which his forefathers had for ages reigned.

There is something romantic in this incident of the child of a Saxon king having to fly to his father's enemies for shelter, and in being indebted to those whom his own countrymen had rendered all but homeless, for his life. Ethelfrith, however, had at one period desolated more British districts than any of his predecessors, and in proportion as he was hated by the Cymry, so would they endeavour to cherish an object armed with such claims as Edwin's, in the hope of one day seeing him a leader, and at their head, when again they measured swords with their old enemies.

But this they were not destined to witness, nor were they able to protect the young king when he grew up, for Ethelfrith was ever in pursuit of him – the figure of the stripling Edwin seemed to stand up between him and the kingdom of Deiri, as if he felt that, whilst the son of Ella was alive, he but sat insecurely in the midst of his new territory.

For several years Edwin was compelled to wander about from province to province, keeping both his name and rank a secret, and trusting to strangers to protect him, as if he feared that the emissaries of Ethelfrith were ever at his heels – until even his existence seems to have been a burden to him, and he doubtless many a time cursed the hour that ever he was born the son of a king. From infancy had his life been sought, by one who ought to have defended him when he was left a helpless child, and heir to the possessions his father had won by conquest – by murder; for sorry we are, as true historians, to state that not a Saxon king throughout the whole British dominions could trace his origin to any other source: nor had William the Norman, on a later day, any better claim to the British crown.

The title of royalty was ever in ancient times written with a red hand. Thank Heaven that it is no longer so, nor has the brow which a golden crown encircles, any need now to be first bathed in human blood.

Edwin is somehow endeared to us, through having descended from that king whose name attracted the attention of monk Gregory in the slave-market of Rome, when he was first struck by the beauty of those British children; for they came from the Deiri, the kingdom which he governed, whose name called forth the

Allelujah to which the good monk, in the joyousness of his heart, as he saw the figure of Hope glimmering brightly in the far distance, gave utterance.

From childhood, Edwin's life seems to have been a romance, and many a painful feeling must he have endured whilst sheltering amongst the Britons in Wales, who were then writhing beneath the oppression of their Saxon conquerors. Allusions to his own father, or his kindred, or curses heaped upon his countrymen, must ever have been issuing from the lips of the humbled Cymry; and who can tell but that to avoid these painful feelings, he set out alone – a stranger amid strangers.

And when weary of this wandering life, he at last threw himself upon the generosity of Redwald, king of East Anglia, who was at that time honoured with the proud title of the *bretwalda* of Britain, as Ethelbert of Kent had been before. Edwin acquainted him with his secret, and Redwald promised to protect him.

But his hiding place was soon known to Ethelfrith, who lost no time in sending messengers to Redwald, first with the offer of rich presents, then with threats: and when he found that neither persuasion nor bribes were effective, he determined to wage war against the king of East Anglia, unless he at once gave up Edwin.

Redwald at last wavered, for in almost every battle the Northumbrian king had been victorious; nor would he probably have seized upon the Deiri, in the face of six powerful Saxon sovereigns, but for the consciousness of the strength he possessed, and the terror attached to his name. The East Anglian king at last reluctantly promised to surrender his guest.

Edwin had a friend in Redwald's court who made him acquainted with the danger that awaited him, and urged him at once to escape. But the poor exile, weary of the miserable existence he had so long led, and the many privations he had endured, refused to fly for his life.

> "If I am to perish," said the young king, "he that destroys me will be disgraced, and not myself. I have made a compact with Redwald that I will not break. And whither should I fly, after having wandered through so many provinces in Britain without finding a shelter? How can I escape my persecutor?"

His friend was silent, and left Edwin to sit alone and brood over his own thoughts. Night came and found the sorrowful king still sitting upon the same cold stone beside the palace, where he appears to have fallen asleep, and to have dreamt that a strange

figure approached him, placed his hand upon his head, and bade him to remember that sign; after having caused him to make several promises as to what he would do in future, if restored to his kingdom, the stranger seemed to depart, having first held out hopes that he should conquer his enemies, and recover the territory of Deiri.

There was nothing very wonderful in such a dream, beyond the fact that it should afterwards become true; and, although we cannot go so far as the venerable chronicler Bede, in the belief that some spirit had appeared to the young king – still, dreams and visions are so interwoven with the sleep that resembles death, and seem, somehow, more allied with the shadows which we believe to people another state of existence, that we can easily imagine, at that dark period, how firm must have been the reliance of our forefathers upon the phantoms which were thus conjured up, by the continuation of such a train of waking thoughts.

Such miracles as the early monkish historians devoutly believed in, the boldest writer would scarcely venture to include in a book professedly dealing with only the wildest subjects of fiction. Yet there are those who think it an act of dishonesty to pass over the dreams, visions, and miracles of the early ages, and that it demonstrates a want of faith not to believe in them now, as our forefathers did in the olden times.

They might as well insist upon our copying out the recipes from such old works as were to be found in the closets of our grandmothers many generations ago; and adopting all the spells and charms therein recorded, as invaluable cures for almost every disease under the sun. What we look upon as firm faith in one age, and believe to be such, we treat as the weakest folly in another, without in either case outraging reason, or bringing to the investigation an uncharitable spirit. For past credulity, a sigh or a smile are enough to mark our pity or censure, but to be partakers of the same belief are thoughts against which the common understanding rebels, even much as we may love the marvellous. A dream is not a miracle, nor is the fulfilment of it a proof of the intercession of the Almighty.

The young king had found favour in the eyes of the queen of East Anglia, and she reasoned with Redwald, and told him how base an act it would be to give up their guest to the man who, having robbed him of his kingdom, now sought to take away his life.

"A king should not violate his faith for gold," she said,
"for good faith is his noblest ornament."

Redwald's heart seems ever to have guided him well when he refused fear into the counsel, so he nobly resolved, instead of giving up his guest, to fight for him, and in place of basely selling his life, to win him back the province he had been driven from. With this resolve, he doubtless felt himself more worthy of the title of the *bretwalda* of Britain.

We regret that Time has not even spared us the name of this noble Saxon queen, that we might add one more woman to the list of these angelic immortals, who stand like stars upon the brow of the deep midnight, that then hung so darkly above the clouded cliffs of Albion. Once Redwald had decided, he began to act; he waited not to be attacked, but, with such forces as he could muster, rushed at once to the boundary of the Deiri.

He met Ethelfrith, before he was prepared for his arrival, on the banks of the river Idel, near Retford in Nottinghamshire, which was a portion of the kingdom he had wrested from Edwin.

Redwald had his guest, his honour, and his kingdom to fight for: Edwin fought for his life, and for the possessions he had inherited from his father.

Ethelfrith had a long-cherished vengeance to appease; a kingdom he had seized upon without anyone having before dared to dispute his claim; and all of East Anglia, now a fair prize, if he could but win it. He had an unworthy cause, yet not any doubt about obtaining the victory, for he had many a time driven the Picts and Scots, with whole hosts of the Cymry, banded together, before him, further to the north than any other than the Romans had ever before done.

His dreams had never been disturbed by the thought of defeat, even when the monks of Bangor were praying against him. He conquered and drove the British kings before him like withered leaves before a storm when yellow Autumn is waning into Winter. No Christian fire had ever burnt upon his pagan altars – to Woden, the god of battles, his sacrifices had always been offered up.

Redwald, more vacillating, kept two altars in the temple in which he worshipped – one dedicated to the grim idol which his warriors still believed in; and the other where he at times knelt beside his fair queen, and sent up his wavering prayers, between the shrine of Woden, and the True God. No truer picture was probably ever drawn of the state of these truly pagan and half-Christian Saxons in the early times, than is here presented; that mingled fear of offending Woden, while the heart yearned for the love of Him whom they believed to be the Giver of all good, for 'God' and 'good' were in their language the same.

Before commencing the battle, Redwald divided his forces into three divisions. One of these he placed under the command of his son Rainer, and the wing which the young prince headed commenced the attack.

Ethelfrith commanded his veteran forces to dash at once into the centre of the enemy's line; and so suddenly and unexpectedly was this manœuvre accomplished, that it was like the instantaneous bursting of a thunder-storm down some steep hill side, covered over with the tall and yellow-waving corn of summer, through which the torrent and the tempest cut a path, for so was the division under prince Rainer dispersed, driven aside and cut asunder, that before the two bodies led on by Redwald and Edwin had time to wheel round, and check the force of that mighty avalanche, the prince was slain, and scarcely a warrior, who but a few moments before had charged so cheerfully under his war-cry remained alive.

For a few moments the terrible tide of battle rolled backward, seeming to recoil from beneath the very force with which it had broken, as if the vanward waves but rushed again upon those that followed, to be driven on with greater might upon the desolated and wreck-strewn beach. Back again was the overwhelming tide borne with mightier force, and thrown off in a spray of blood from the points of ten thousand unflinching weapons, while Redwald himself, with lowering brow, and lip compressed, strode sullenly onward, and hewed his way into the very heart of the contest.

Ethelfrith, outstripping his followers, rushed headlong into the very centre of the battle; the gap he had hewn with his own powerful arm closed behind him, and there stood between him and the remains of his army an impenetrable wall of the enemy. And here he fell, the last billow of the battle broke, for the companion waves had rolled out far to seaward, and only the shore over which they had broken was left, strewn over with the wrecks of the slain.

Death had at last done his mighty work; under his dark and awful banner, Edwin had distinguished himself; those gloomy gates had opened the way to the kingdom from which he had so long been driven.

And so with the assistance of Redwald, he not only became the king of the Deira, but also conquered the broad provinces of Bernicia, driving before him the sons of Ethelfrith, and taking the title of the sole king of Northumbria, for he united under his sway the kingdoms which Ida had governed, and Ella, his father, had won. Thus, the youth who had so long been a wanderer and an exile, who scarcely knew where to fly for shelter, and who was ever in fear of his life, became at last the undisputed monarch of two mighty and now combined Saxon kingdoms, the Deira and Bernicia.

Edwin no sooner found himself firmly seated on the throne of Northumbria, than he sent into Kent, and solicited the hand of Edilburga in marriage. She was the daughter of the late Ethelbert, so distinguished for his kindness to the Christian missionaries. Probably Edwin had become acquainted with her while he wandered 'homeless, amid a thousand homes'.

Her brother Eadbald had, by this time, become a Christian, had cast aside his heathen idols and pagan altars, and established himself beside the church at Canterbury, which had long been the metropolis of Kent. Eadbald justly argued that it was wrong for a Christian maiden to become the wife of a pagan husband, of one who could neither share with her the holy sacrament, nor kneel down to worship before the altar of the same Holy God.

Edwin bound himself by a solemn promise that he would offer no obstacle to the royal lady following her own faith, and that all who accompanied her, whether women, priests, or laymen, should have full liberty to follow their own form of religion; and that if, upon close examination by the wise and good men of his own faith, he found the Christian creed better than that of Odin, he might at last adopt it.

The Saxon princess had the fullest confidence in the promises of the pagan king, and with a long train of noble and lowly attendants, headed by Paulinus, who was by this time a bishop, she left the home of her fathers in Kent, and as Rowena had previously done, went to sojourn among strangers. Many a prayer was offered up by the way, and the holy rites of the church to which she belonged were daily celebrated.

Timidly must the maiden's heart have beaten when she first set foot within that pagan land; but she probably also remembered the time when many of her father's subjects were idolaters.

Nothing for the first year seems to have ruffled the smooth course of love between the pagan king and his Christian queen. Paulinus continued to preach, but made no converts; and the love of Edilburga, and worship of Odin, went on together hand in hand; for though Edwin himself listened to the music of lips as

sweet as those of Bertha, which had murmured conversion into the ears of Ethelbert, yet his creed remained unchanged. He loved, listened, and sighed, yet his heathen faith remained unshaken.

It was at the holy time of Easter, while Edwin was seated in his palace beside the Derwent, that a messenger suddenly arrived from Cwichhelm, the pagan king of Wessex, and sought an audience, to make known his mission. He was, of course, admitted.

While kneeling to deliver his message, the stranger suddenly started up, drew forth a dagger which was concealed under his dress, and was in the act of rushing upon the king, when Lilla, a thane in attendance, threw himself, in a moment, between the body of the monarch and the assassin – just in that brief interval of time which elapsed between the uplifting and the descending of the weapon; yet with such force was the deadly blow driven home, that the dagger passed clean through the body of Lilla, and slightly wounded the king. Although the swords of the attendants were instantly drawn, yet the assassin was not cut down until he had stabbed another knight with the dagger, which he had drawn from the body of the faithful thane who so nobly sacrificed his life to save that of the king.

That same evening (it was Easter Sunday), Edilburga gave birth to a daughter; the event was probably hastened by the shock the murderer had occasioned. Edwin gave thanks to Odin for the birth of his child; and when Paulinus again drew his attention to the God who had so miraculously preserved his life, he promised he would follow the new faith which the bishop was so anxious to convert him to – if he was victorious over the king of Wessex, who had sent out his emissary to destroy him. Edwin further consented that his daughter should be baptized, as a sign of his good faith. Several other members of his household were at the same time united to the Christian church.

The account of Edwin's campaign against the king of Wessex is so vague and uncertain that we are compelled to pass it over altogether. It appears, however, that he slew his enemy and returned home victorious; but still he delayed his baptism, although he abandoned his idol-worship, and would often be seen sitting alone, as if holding serious communion with himself; still, he was undecided as to whether or not to change his ancient faith.

He also held long and frequent conversations with Paulinus, and had many serious discussions with his own nobles. He was even honoured with a letter from the pope, urging him to abandon his idols. Edilburga also received a letter from the same high authority, pointing out her duty to do all that she could, by her intercession, to hasten his conversion; but Edwin still remained unchanged.

The stormy halls of Odin and the boisterous revels in which the spirits of the departed warriors were believed to partake were more congenial to the martial hearts of the Saxons, than the peace, humility, and gentleness which clothed the Christian religion. A vision or a miracle is again called in by the venerable Bede to complete the conversion of Edwin. This we shall pass over without openly expressing any feeling of doubt or disbelief.

The means which the Almighty might take to bring about the conversion of a heathen nation are beyond the comprehension of man. We doubt not the light which fell upon and surrounded Saul, when breathing slaughter against the Christians whilst he was on his way to Damascus, for there we at once acknowledge the wonder-working hand of God.

It required no such powerful agency for Paulinus to become acquainted with Edwin's previous dream. Nor does there appear to have been anything miraculous in the token which the king was reminded of; neither was the incident at all so startling as it first appears to be, for he had beyond doubt made Edilburga acquainted with the subject of his dream, and what would not a woman do, to accomplish the conversion of a husband she loved? Even after all, Edwin assembled his nobles and counsellors together openly, to discuss the new religion before he was baptized, for the vision or miracle had not yet dispelled his doubts.

When Edwin assembled his pagan priests and nobles together, and threw open before them the whole subject, Coifi, who had long administered the rites at the altar of Odin, and, as it appears, reaped but little benefit, thus spoke out, plainly and feelingly, at once. (We trust that Edilburga was not present.)

> "You see, O King, what is now preached to us; I declare to you most truly, what I have most certainly experienced, that the religion which we have hitherto professed, contains no virtue at all, nor any utility. Not one of your whole court has been more attentive to the worship of your gods than myself, although many have received richer benefits, greater honours, and have prospered more than I have done. Now, if these gods had been of any real use, would they not have assisted me, instead of them? If, then, after due inquiry, you see that these 'new things' which they tell us of will be better, let us have them without any delay."

Coifi was weary of waiting for the good things which stood ready prepared for him in the halls of Valhalla; he wanted to have a foretaste whilst living.

But we will leave plain-spoken Coifi to introduce the next orator, who was one of Nature's poets, though a pagan; and the passage is doubly endeared to us, by the knowledge that on a later day, Alfred the Great translated it, word for word and letter for letter. We regret that we cannot give the original, for there are many words in it which seem out of place, such as we believe the eloquent orator never uttered, although Bede lived about this time, and probably heard it from the lips of someone who was present when it was spoken. It ran nearly as follows:

> "The life of man while here, O King, seems to me, when I think of that life which is to come, and which we know not of, like a scene at one of your own winter feasts. When you sit in your hall with the blaze of the fire in the midst of it, and round you your thanes and ealdermen, and the whole hall is bright with the warmth, and while storms of rain and snow are heard out in the cold air, in comes a small sparrow at one door, and flies round our feast; then it goes out another way into the cold. While it is in, it feels not the winter storm, but is warm, and feels a comfort while it stays; but when out in the winter cold, from whence it came, it goes far from our eyes. Such is here the life of man. It acts and thinks while here, but what it did when we saw it not, we do not know, nor do we know what it will do when it is gone."

He then finished by adding something about the new religion, and prayed of them to adopt it, if it was more worthy of their belief, and opened clearer views respecting a future state than the old.

Paulinus was present, and when he had satisfactorily answered all questions, a fearful feeling still seemed to linger amongst the pagans, as to who should first desecrate their old temple, and overthrow the idols and altars before which they had so long worshipped.

"Give me a horse and a spear," said Coifi, "and I will."

They were brought to him. We cannot help picturing Coifi in his eagerness to get rid of the old religion, nor how Paulinus, with his dark hair, hooked nose, swarthy countenance, and darker eyes, just looked for a moment at Edwin, as the pagan priest hurled his spear at the idol temple, and profaned it.

Those who were present would have thought him mad.

What Coifi thought of the people is not on record. He knew what the idols were, better than they did. For day after day, and year after year, he had attended to the shrine, yet received no reward; and doubtless Coifi thought that, let the new religion be what it might, it could not be worse than the old one.

When he had hurled his spear against the temple, it was profaned, and could never more be dedicated to the worship of Odin; for such an act was held impious by the ancient Saxon pagans. The building was then destroyed, and the surrounding enclosures levelled to the ground.

This scene took place near the Derwent, not far from the spot where Edwin had so narrow an escape from the assassin Eumer. In Bede's time it was called Godmundham, or 'the home of the gods'.

After this, Edwin and his nobility were baptized, and through his persuasion, the son of his protector, Redwald, embraced Christianity, and diffused it amongst his subjects in East Anglia.

Edwin himself, as we have shown, had in his younger days been a wanderer and an exile; and although we have no account of the privations he endured, they were doubtless great, and perhaps we should not much err in surmising that many a time he had endured the pangs of hunger and thirst: for on a later day he caused stakes to be fastened beside the highways wherever a clear spring was to be found, and to these posts, brazen dishes were chained, to enable the weary and thirsty traveller to refresh himself. For houses were then few and far apart, and the wayfarer had often to journey many a dreary league before he could obtain refreshment, as the monasteries were the only places in which he could halt and rest. In Edwin's reign, and through his kingdom, it is said that a woman with an infant at her breast might walk from the Tweed to the Trent without fearing injury from any one. He seems to have been beloved by all, and Edilburga ever moved beside him like a ministering angel.

But Edwin was not destined to go down peaceably to his grave; some quarrel arose between him and the son of his old Welsh host, Cadvan: what the cause was, we do not know; but it led to a severe battle, and as it was fought near Morpeth, it is evident that the Welsh king was the invader.

THE BAPTISM OF EDWIN

Edwin was, as usual, victorious, and chased Cadwallon into Wales. Some time after this event, there sprang up a renowned pagan warrior amongst the Saxons, named Penda, who governed the kingdom of Mercia, a portion of Britain that up to this period scarcely attracts the historian's attention. This Mercian king, Cadwallon prevailed upon to unite his forces with his own, and attack the Northumbrian monarch.

The battle is believed to have taken place at Hatfield Chase, in Yorkshire, at the close of autumn in the year 633. King Edwin was slain, together with one of his sons, Osfrid. Most of his army perished – a clear proof of the bitter struggle.

Cadwallon and his ally Penda overran the united kingdoms of Northumbria, desolating the Deiri and Bernicia in their march, and spreading terror everywhere.

Edilburga escaped with her children into Kent; Paulinus accompanied her, for the Christian churches appear to have been the chief objects which the Mercian monarch sought to destroy. The world seemed to have nothing for Edilburga after the death of her royal husband. Her brother, Eadbald, the king of Kent, received her kindly and sorrowfully. The widowed queen, by his consent, built a monastery at Liming and afterwards took the veil.

*

Such was the end of the beautiful daughter of Ethelbert, she who as a young girl had many a time seen Augustine at her father's court, and doubtless looked with childish wonder on the holy banner which the missionaries bore before them, whereon the image of the Blessed Redeemer was portrayed, when they first appeared in Kent.

Upon the death of Edwin, the kingdom of Northumbria was again divided. Osric, a descendant of Ella, ascended the throne of the Deiri, and Eanfrid, the son of Ethelfrith, whom Edwin had driven into exile, reigned over Bernicia.

Osric soon perished, for Cadwallon still continued his ravages, and while the king of Deiri was besieging a strong fortress which the Welsh monarch occupied, an unexpected sally was made, and in the skirmish Osric was slain.

Eanfrid met with a less glorious death. While he was within the camp of Cadwallon, suing for peace, he was, even against all the acknowledged laws of that barbarous age, put to death. This Welsh king appears to have been as great a scourge to the Saxons as ever king Arthur was in his day; nor does his old ally, Penda, seem to have been a jot less sparing of his own countrymen – but his doings will form the subject of our next chapter.

Cadwallon is said to have fought in fourteen battles and sixty skirmishes, and so odious was the last year in which he distinguished himself – so blotted by his ravages and the apostasy of many of the Saxon kings, that Bede says that the annalists, by one consent, refused to record the reigns of these renegades, so added it to the sovereignty of Oswald.

The most important event that we have to record in his reign was the victory he obtained over Cadwallon, which occurred soon after he was seated upon the throne of Bernicia. Oswald was already celebrated for his piety, and previous to his battle with the Welsh king, he planted the image of the cross upon the field, holding it with his own hands, while his soldiers filled up the hollow which they had made in the earth to receive it. When the cross was firmly secured, he exclaimed,

> "Let us all bend our knees, and with one heart and voice pray to the True and the Living God, that He in His mercy will defend us from a proud and cruel enemy: for to Him it is known that we have commenced this war, for the salvation and safety of our people."

All knelt, as he had commanded, around the cross, and when the last murmur of the solemn prayer had died away, they marched onward with stout hearts to meet the terrible enemy. Of the battle we have scarcely any other record than that which briefly relates the death of Cadwallon and the destruction of his army. The spot in which the cross was planted was called 'Heavenfield', and was for ages afterwards held in great reverence.

But neither the piety of Oswald, nor his victory over the Welsh king, could protect him from the wrath of Penda: and the scene of our history now shifts to the kingdom of Mercia, which, up to this time, had seemed to sleep in the centre of the Saxon dominions: for those who had settled down in the midland districts had, with the exception of Crida, scarcely left so much as a name behind, and he is known only as the grandfather of Penda.

To the deeds of the latter we have now arrived – and he who assisted in slaying five kings is the next stormy spirit that throws its shadow upon our pages.

14 PENDA, THE PAGAN MONARCH OF MERCIA

> The gates of mercy shall be all shut up:
> And the fleshed soldier, rough and hard of heart,
> In liberty of bloody hand, shall range
> With conscience wide as hell: mowing like grass
> Your fresh fair virgins and your flowering infants.
>
> – Shakspeare

Until now, the kingdom of Mercia has scarcely attracted our attention, but the time at last came when it was destined to rise, under the sovereignty of Penda, and with a startling distinctiveness, above the rest of the Saxon states.

As the midland counties bordered upon the Deiri, it is not improbable that Mercia had been subject to the sway of the more northern monarchs, until the grandson of Crida appeared, and, struck by its fallen state, resolved at once to raise it to its true dignity. We have seen him before, when he figured in the battle where he joined Cadwallon, and overthrew the once-powerful Edwin; then he gained but an empty victory.

He now resolved to retrace his steps and reap a more substantial harvest, or perish in the attempt. More than sixty years had already rolled over his head, yet for military skill and talent he had scarcely an equal, and when, ten years before, he was crowned king of Mercia, many foresaw that his would be a terrible reign; he had linked himself with the British – daringly thrown down his gauntlet and challenged all comers; no one was found bold enough to pick it up.

Wherever he appeared, Mercy fled with a shiver, and Hope placed her fair hands before her eyes to weep: from step to step did he advance as he grew grey in crime, still glorying in the hoariness of his iniquities. Bold, ambitious, and cruel, he sought out danger wherever it was to be found, and attacked Power in the very heart of his stronghold; he knew only Mercy by the name of Death, nor shunned he the fate to which he consigned others. He hated not the Christians who adhered rigidly to the tenets of their new creed, but if they halted between two opinions, he abhorred them; while on his part he worshipped Odin, and never left the altars of his grim war-god dry for want of a victim.

Endowed with a strong and fearless mind, and a body that age only seemed to harden, he led the way from battle to battle, and victory to victory, while the neighbouring kings looked on and trembled. It was no marvel that such a conqueror found ready allies amongst the Cymry, or that they were ever eager to join him when he required their aid, while he in return seems to have stood ready armed for any cause that might chance to fall in his way. But for his assistance to Cadwallon, Edwin might probably have died an old man in his bed, with Edilburga and his children kneeling beside him.

But ambition was the rock on which nearly all these ancient kings were wrecked; the open ocean was not wide enough for them; wherever it was rumoured that danger lurked, there they at once steered – they deemed it cowardly to wait for the coming of death, so seized the helm and sailed boldly out to look for his dark dominions. To be chained to the domestic hearth was to them a misery. The bark of the old hound, the recognising flutter of the familiar hawk, and the prattle of children all became tiresome.

Old household affections palled; Edilburga might smile, and Paulinus pray, but the tramp of the war-horse, and the ringing of the sword upon the buckler, and the clang of the battle-axe, as it cleaved its way through helmet and armour, were sweeter sounds than these; the spirit within yearned for the sleep which was purchased by a dearly won victory; even the eyes of grey-headed old men brightened when the contest was talked over in which they had fought, and they went out of the hall, tottering at every step, to bask in the sunshine, and sigh over deeds done. Wearisome was the morning light to their eyes, when it dawned not upon the tented field; they loved better to see the banner of the red dragon of the Britons waving upon some distant height, opposite to which their own standard of the white horse fluttered, than to watch the motion of the trees, or the rustle of the yellow corn, or to hear the bleating and the lowing of the cattle upon a thousand hills: to such belonged Penda, the ruler of Mercia.

Whether the death of Cadwallon, the British king with whom Penda's forces were allied when Edwin was defeated at the battle of Hatfield-chase, caused the Mercian monarch to invade Bernicia, to revenge his fall and defeat, or whether the love of conquest alone induced Penda to undertake this expedition, is not recorded. Neither is it whether he was present at the battle in which Cadwallon was slain.

Whatever his motives, he attacked and slew Oswald, without any apparent cause of quarrel, and in him perished one of the best of the Northern kings. It is said that while the barbed javelin which caused his death was still fixed in his breast, he never for a moment ceased to pray; and that for centuries after his death, his name was ever linked with the following pious sentence he uttered when he fell: "May the Lord have mercy on their souls!"

It is also recorded of Oswald that one day, as he was about to partake of the refreshments which were placed before him on a silver dish, the almoner, whose office it was to relieve the poor, stepped in and informed him that a number of beggars were waiting, without soliciting alms. When his eye alighted upon the rich vessel in which the dainties were piled, the thoughts of their wants, and his own unnecessary luxuries, rose before him with so striking a contrast, that he ordered the untouched food to be distributed amongst the beggars, and the silver dish to be broken up and given to them. Penda caused the head and limbs of this pious and charitable king to be severed from the body, transfixed on stakes, and exposed to the public gaze.

He then marched through Northumbria, spreading death and desolation wherever he trod; attacked the castle of Bamborough, and, unable to carry it by storm, demolished all the buildings in the neighbourhood, and piled up the wood and thatch around the strong fortress, and then set fire to the ruins he had heaped together. Fortunately for the besieged, the wind changed just as the flames began to rise, and the eddying gust blew back the blazing ruins upon the besiegers.

Penda then turned his back upon Northumbria. We next meet him in Wessex, where he makes war upon Cenwalch, for some insult the latter had offered to Penda's sister; Cenwalch is driven out of his kingdom, remains in exile three years, and then returns, having apparently reconciled himself to the Mercian king.

When he had finished his work in Wessex, and Sigebert had resigned his crown, he directed his steps to East Anglia, for Redwald had long since slept with his fathers: he had also founded a school, from which it is not improbable the present University of Cambridge sprung; and having given his kingdom to his kinsman Ecgric, and built a monastery, into which he at last retired, he had long since taken a farewell of all his greatness.

But Sigebert had been renowned in his day; and now danger was knocking at the door, the East Anglians were unwilling that an old warrior should be pattering his prayers when he ought to be wielding his battle-axe; and it is recorded that his former subjects drew him forcibly out of the monastery, and compelled him to lead them on against Penda. With only a white wand in his hand, and probably robed in his monkish habiliments, the old soldier took the command of the battle.

His religious scruples, however, preventing him from using any warlike weapon. We can almost picture him, pale with his ascetic life, for no one had adhered more rigidly to the monastic rules than he had done, standing with his white wand uplifted amid a throng of warriors, pointing to the most salient points of the opposing army, with a martial glimmer just lighting up for a moment the cold grey eye which for years had only contemplated that glory which he hoped to enjoy beyond the grave.

We can imagine the sudden contrast of sounds – from the low muttered prayer, the holy hymns chanted within the walls of his monastery – to the shout, the rush, the struggle, and the clanging of arms. Nor is it difficult to picture the look of contempt with which the pagan king Penda would gaze upon his ghostly opponent, or to imagine the bitter jeers to which the hardened heathen would give utterance as he wiped his bloody battle-axe, and gazed upon the monk-king and his crowned kinsman, as they lay together amid the slain – for both Sigebert and Ecgric fell, and their whole army was routed or slaughtered by the hitherto invincible Penda.

Anna succeeded Ecgric and Sigebert; but scarcely was he seated upon the perilous throne of East Anglia, before the pagan warrior again made his appearance; for although Penda was now an old man, grey-headed, and eighty years of age, he could no more live without fighting than he could without food.

Anna had been guilty of sheltering Cenwalch, the king of Wessex, after Penda had dethroned him; an unpardonable offence in the eyes of the hoary old heathen; so he marched once more into East Anglia, and slew him. He had by this time sent five kings and thousands of their followers as offerings to Odin, and not yet satisfied, he resolved once more to visit the northern kingdoms, for the pleasant vallies which stretched on either side the Trent had no charms for Penda. The 'thirty-armed river', as Milton has called it, could not retain him within its boundaries; he liked not the air of our midland counties, so he set off to pay another visit to the Deiri or Bernicia, with every mile of which he was doubtless familiar.

He had grown grey in fighting battles, had been a king thirty years, and during the whole period was either preparing to attack, or marching, or fighting. The old chroniclers compare him to a vulture, a wild beast, ravenous for prey, and one whose chief delight was in the clashing of arms, and the shedding of human blood.

After having slain Oswald and brutally exhibited his remains, he appears to have paid frequent visits to Oswy, who succeeded him. But Oswy had no disposition to fight, and therefore endeavoured to keep the quarrelsome old Mercian quiet by exhausting the Northumbrian treasury. Growling like a tiger, Penda refused to accept all the treasures he could heap together; he was neither to be bought over by gold, nor prayers. He came to fight, and fight he would; he seemed like a drunken man who is determined to quarrel, even if he has to run his head against the first post he meets with. He had come, he said, to extirpate the whole race of the Northumbrians – the Deiri, Bernicia, and all – he had come to kill.

When Oswy found that all entreaties were in vain, he mustered his forces together, which were far inferior to Penda's in number. Before commencing the battle, Oswy vowed, like Jephthah of old, that if he obtained the victory, he would dedicate his daughter to the service of the Lord; and having formed this resolution, he issued forth to meet the mighty man-slayer, who had hitherto scarcely sustained a single defeat.

The Northumbrian, with a heavy heart, divided the command of his little army between himself and his son Alfred. The battle took place somewhere in Yorkshire, but the exact location cannot with certainty be pointed out; it was in the neighbourhood of a river, and not far distant from York. The contest was terrible; the army under the command of Penda appears to have been made up of Britons and Saxons, some of whom were dragged reluctantly into the battle, and who waited the first favourable moment to turn their arms against the dreaded chieftain.

The low land in the rear of Penda's army was flooded; beyond, the deep-swollen river was already roaring as if in expectation of its prey. Penda charged as usual – hot, eager, and impetuous, as if the victory was already his own; but the old man's arms were not so strong as they had been. He could not see his way so clearly as he had done beforetime.

Odilwald, who occupied a favourable position, had not yet stirred a step. It seems as if one portion of Penda's mighty force was jealous of another; there was the river roaring behind, and Oswy bearing down upon them before.

Midway all was confusion, and in the midst of it stood Penda, blinded with fury, and bleeding from his wounds. Over the dying and the dead trampled the victorious army of Oswy. Over Penda they trod, who lay upon the ground a hideous mass, his grey head cloven open by a blow from a battle-axe. None paused to survey him.

Before the Northumbrians the routed host rushed onward, onward, until the ringing of armour, and the clashing of blade upon blade, sunk into a gurgle, and a moan, and a splash; and still the river tore on its way, as if in haste to make room for more. Downward the defeated plunged, into deep beds, where the hungry pike slept, and the slimy eel lay coiled. The flooded fields were manured with the dead; hideous sights which many a rich harvest has since covered; the river-bed was clogged up with the bodies of the slain, which fishes fed upon, and winter rains at last washed away – rich relics to pave the floor of that gloomy hall, where Hela the terrible reigned.

If ever there was a clattering of skulls in Valhalla it was then. If Odin ever rushed out with open arms, to meet the bloodiest of his worshippers, it was when the soul of Penda came. What a crimson country is ours! What rivers of gore has it taken to make our green England what it is! It is no marvel that even the rims of our daisies are dyed crimson by contact with such a blood-soaked soil.

Oswy, after this unexpected victory, now overran Mercia, and subjected it to his sway. His daughter Alchfleda he also gave in marriage to Peada, the son of Penda, and installed him in his father's kingdom, on condition that he should introduce Christianity into his dominions.

Alfred, the son of Oswy, in return married the daughter of Penda, whose name was Cyneburga. Thus on each side a pagan was united to a Christian, and the work of conversion went on prosperously; for there were now but few corners of the British dominions in which the true faith was not introduced.

Such changes were enough to make the stern old Saxon heathen leap out of his grave. In his lifetime, no one would have been found bold enough to have proposed them. Alchfleda's mother was still living, and remained a firm follower of the old idolatrous creed; she seems to have accompanied her daughter into Mercia, and had doubtless in her train many a grey old veteran, who still bowed the knee before the altars of Odin, and who looked upon a religion which taught peace, good will, and charity to all mankind, with disdain.

It is not known by whose instigation Peada was assassinated. Both his wife and her mother stand accused of the deed, but no cause is assigned for the former perpetrating so dreadful a crime; nor can any other reason be assigned for the latter having done it, beyond what we have given. Peada, however, fell at the holy time of Easter, which seems to have been a favourite season for assassination amongst the pagan Saxons, in proof of which numerous instances

might be quoted.

Before his death, Peada commenced the famous monastery of Peterborough, which his brother Wulfhere completed. Nor was Wulfhere content with only finishing the minster, for he gave to the Abbot Saxulf, to the monks, and their successors for ever, and all the lands and waters, meads, fens, and weirs, which lay for many miles around it, and covered in extent what forms more than one English shire.

Wulfhere, like Sigebert, appears to have been as much of a monk as a warrior, though a little of old Penda's blood still flowed in his veins; and when Cenwalch, of Wessex, who had been humbled and disgraced by Penda, resolved to have his revenge upon the son, although he was at first successful, the Mercians at last became conquerors, and Cenwalch was again exiled, and his kingdom fell into the hands of the Mercian sovereign.

The king of Essex, about this time, made frequent visits to Oswy's court, and the Northumbrian sovereign lost no opportunity of dissuading him from following his idol worship. The arguments Oswy used, though simple, were convincing; he told him that such objects as were fashioned out of stone or wood, and which the axe or the fire could so readily destroy and consume, could not contain a Godhead. Such reasoning had the desired effect, and the king of Essex, together with numbers of his subjects, abandoned their pagan belief.

The sovereign of Sussex was also converted through the instrumentality of Wulfhere, who was as eager to spread the doctrines of Christianity as his father had ever been to uphold the worship of Woden. Cenwalch, the king of Wessex, who, like so many others about this period, keeps crossing the busy stage at intervals, only to fill up the scenes, at length died, but whether in exile or not is uncertain.

Saxburga, the widowed queen, stepped into the vacant throne; but the Wessex nobles refused to be governed by a woman, although she wielded the sceptre with a firmer hand, and ruled the kingdom better than her husband had ever done; strengthening her forces, and ever holding herself in readiness in case of an invasion.

Still there was ever someone amongst her nobles who shared her rule; and one of these, a descendant from the renowned Cerdric, led her forces against the king of Mercia. Essex was at this time under the sway of Wulfhere, and it is likely enough that he looked with a jealous eye upon the bold front which Saxburga's kingdom presented, after the death of Cenwalch, who had been so frequently conquered.

WULFHERE THE KIND-HEARTED

A battle was fought in Wiltshire, in which neither party appear to have reaped any material advantage; and in little more than a year after the contest, both the leaders were in their graves.

Oswy, the conqueror of Penda, had before this died, and his son Ecgfrid became the king of Northumbria, in which the Deiri and Bernicia were now united.

Alfred, who had married Penda's daughter, after having aided in destroying her father and his powerful army at the battle in Yorkshire, was not allowed to succeed Oswy, on account of some flaw in his birth. Nearly all beside, of any note, who figured in this busy period, had passed away, except the last son of Penda, named Ethelred, who, after the death of Wulfhere, ascended the Mercian throne.

Ecgfrid fell in a battle against the Picts, though not before he had invaded Mercia, for although Ethelred had married his sister, it seemed as if the hostile blood which had so long flowed between the sons, Oswy and Penda, was not to be blended by marriage. The archbishop Theodore stepped in between the combatants, and healed up the breach long before Ecgfrid perished.

About this time, also, died Cadwaladyr, the last of the Cymry who aspired to the sovereignty of Britain. His death was the cause of a battle being fought.

Similar unimportant events make up the catalogue which closes the account of this period. The Saxon kingdoms seemed to stand upon an ever-moving earthquake: one was swallowed to-day, and cast up again on the morrow: the earth was ever rocking and reeling: kings came and went as the images shift in a kaleidoscope.

If one year saw a sovereign victorious, the next beheld him dethroned and an exile; he put on his crown, or laid it aside, just as his more powerful neighbour bade him. When fortune placed him uppermost, he retaliated in the same way on his former conqueror.

Still we have before us the stirring times of Offa the Terrible; Egbert and Ethelwulf followed by the stormy sea-kings, whose invasions were more merciless than those of the Saxons; for the history of this period is like an ocean studded with islands, some of which lie near together, others wide apart. Many which, from the distance, seem to have a barren and forbidding look, are, on a nearer approach, found rich in ancient remains; and though now silent and desolate, we discover in what is left behind traces of the once mighty inhabitants that ages ago have passed away.

Such is the history of the early Saxon kingdoms. Where an idle voyager might yawn and grow weary, his intelligent companion would linger, and gaze, and ponder in silent wonder and reverential awe.

15 DECLINE OF THE SAXON OCTARCHY

> Let us sit upon the ground,
> and tell sad stories of the death of kings –
> how some have been deposed, some slain in war;
> some haunted by the ghosts they have deposed;
> some poisoned by their wives, some sleeping killed.
> All murdered – for within the hollow crown
> that rounds the mortal temples of a king,
> keeps Death his court.
>
> – Shakespeare

The remainder of our journey through the kingdoms which anciently formed the Saxon Octarchy now lies in a more direct road. There are fewer of those perplexing paths and winding ways, such as we have hitherto been compelled to thread, in our difficult course through this dimly-discovered country of the past.

We are now on the sun-bright borders of those dark old forest fastnesses, amid which we could scarcely see what flowers were at our feet, or catch a clear glimpse of the outstretched sky that hung above our heads. A few steps from this, and we leave this land of twilight and uncertain shadows behind.

After the death of Ecgfrid, Alfred, who we already know as having fought in the battle in which Penda fell, and afterwards, as having married his daughter, ascended the throne of Northumbria.

We have previously shown how, on account of his birth, his succession was disputed by the nobles. Against their decision, he offered neither defence nor resistance, but applying himself to study, he so enriched his mind, under the instruction of the famous Bishop Wilfrid, that Bede classes him as first amongst the kings of Anglo-Saxons for his literary acquirements.

He "waded not through slaughter to a throne," but calmly abided his time, and when it came, ceased his study to pick up the sceptre. His court was the resort of literary men and enlightened travellers, and Aldhelm, a celebrated scholar of that day, stood high in his favour. There was a firmness about his character worthy of the name which afterwards becomes so endeared to us, for when he could not conscientiously agree in certain matters with his old tutor, Wilfrid, he allowed the bishop to quit his dominions, and neither did a letter from the Pope influence or alter his resolution.

Nothing of note appears to have occurred in Northumbria during his reign; the expulsion of Eadwulf, and the ascension of Osred, were accomplished without difficulty. Ceolwulf came next, to whom Bede dedicated his Ecclesiastical History; but we must not step too suddenly into the familiar light which seems all at once about to break upon us.

Ceadwalla, a descendant of the renowned Cerdric's, after the death of Ecgfrid, made a stand against the nobles of Wessex, who had banished him from that kingdom. He first attacked the king of Sussex, slew him, and desolated his dominions. He then, accompanied by his brother Mollo, made an inroad into Kent, where they ravaged and destroyed the towns and villages for miles around.

While Mollo, with several of his soldiers, were busied in plundering a house, they were surrounded by the enraged men of Kent, who, preventing the escape of the marauders, set fire to the building on every side, and burnt all within alive. The king of Wessex revenged his brother's death, and, far and wide, around the scene of this terrible sacrifice, he made "a land of mourning."

After this he went on a pilgrimage to Rome, was baptized by the Pope, and died the week after.

Ina then ascended the throne of Wessex; his celebrated laws are still in existence, and as they throw considerable light upon the manners of this remote period, we will take a hasty glance at them before proceeding further.

If a child was not baptized within thirty days after its birth, a penalty of thirty shillings was demanded; if that period elapsed and the ceremony was still neglected, the priest or the parents must forfeit all they possessed.

If a slave or theow worked on Sunday by his master's commands, he became free; if a freeman worked on that day, by his own consent, he forfeited his freedom.

If any one sold his servant, whether a slave or a freeman, he must pay his full value.

If a poor man died, and left his wife with a child, six shillings a year was to be paid for its maintenance, together with a cow in the summer, and an ox in winter – its kindred was to take charge of the house until the child became of age.

If a man was killed, his life was valued according to what he was worth, and the slayer had to pay a fixed price for his death.

*

Crude as these laws are, and barbarous as they prove the people to have been for which they were made, still they are the first landmarks, reared in a wild and uncivilized country, which point out to man the extent of his possessions and his power; the first attempt to draw an even line between might and right – for here the poor theow, the slave of the soil, he who was sold like the cattle upon the estate to the next purchaser, felt secure within his allotted mark.

The day of holy rest was his own; if his lord compelled him to labour, the laws of Ina, next day, made him a free man.

Ina, like his predecessors, was compelled to fight his way to peace, and amid his hostilities, he became involved in a war with Ceolred, king of Mercia. His queen appears to have been as courageous as himself, and is said to have besieged one of her husband's enemies at Taunton, and to have levelled to the ground the castle in which he was sheltered.

Ina rebuilt the abbey of Glastonbury, and endowed it with rich gifts. It seems to have become a custom amongst the Saxon kings at this period, to go on pilgrimage to Rome, resign their crowns, and become monks. Ina's queen had long tried, but in vain, to induce her husband to follow what she considered such worthy examples; but her entreaties had hitherto proved useless. She at last hit upon the following device.

A feast had been held in one of Ina's castles; and the morning after the banquet they went out together to ride; when they returned, she conducted Ina into the banqueting hall, which was now covered with filth, and occupied by a herd of swine, a litter of which was resting upon the very couch he had before occupied.

Well might so sudden a change astonish him, and we can readily imagine the dark spot that gathered upon his angry brow.

205

Such a mode of conversion would have startled either Augustine or Paulinus, and made even cunning Coifi pause before he changed his opinion. The queen pleaded guilty to the fault, and reasoned upon the matter as follows:

> "My lord," she said, "this is very different from the noise and hilarity of yesterday; there are no brilliant hangings now; no table weighed down with silver vessels, no delicacies to delight the palate, neither flatterers nor parasites – all these have vanished like the smoke before the wind – have all passed away into nothingness. Ought we not, then, to feel alarmed, who covet them so much, yet are every way as transient? Are not all such things so? and are we not ourselves like a river, that hurries headlong and heedlessly along to the dark and illimitable ocean of time? Unhappy must we ever be if we let such things occupy our minds.
>
> Think, I entreat you, how disgusting those things become of which we are so enamoured; and see what filthy objects we have become attached to; for in those filthy relics we may see what our pampered bodies will at last become. Oh! let us reflect, that the greater we have been, and the more powerful we now are, the more alarmed we ought to be, for the greater will be the punishment of our misconduct."

Ina listened, sighed, resigned his crown, and set off for Rome, where he founded a school, and imposed a tax of a penny upon every family in his kingdom, which was called Romescot, and which went to support the institution he had raised. As a proof of his sincerity, he wore a common dress, lived meanly, cut his hair, laboured hard, and dwelt in retirement with his queen, until he died a 'good old man'.

His brother, Inigils, had died a few years before him, a name that falls silent as snow upon the pages of History; yet like the snow, doing its silent work – for he must have been a man of some note in his day and generation, to have been the father of Egbert and the grandfather of Alfred the Great, from whom descended a long line of kings.

*

The Mercian nobles rose up and put to death Ostrida (or Osthryth), the wife of Ethelred their king, for what cause history is altogether silent; neither the why nor the wherefore is given. The sentence reads in the *Saxon Chronicle* like an epitaph upon a gravestone, yet she was the daughter of the once powerful Oswy of Northumbria, and when killed, was queen of the Mercians. The very mystery which hangs around her fate interests us, and we want to know something about what she had done to suffer such dreadful punishment, but all our  inquiries are vain; beyond the mere entry of her violent death, not even a doubt is registered, for us to pause over.

The deed was done, and is recorded in one brief, terrible sentence, and we know no more.

Her husband, Ethelred, abandoned the crown of Mercia to his nephew Cenred, and entered the monastery of Bardney, as a monk, going through all the routine of common duties, like a humble brother, until at last he became abbot of the monastery which he himself had founded.

Ethelbald is the next king of Mercia who commands our attention. He had been nursed in the stern school of privation; like Edwin of Northumbria, he

207

had been persecuted in his youth, and owed his life to Guthlac, the hermit of Croyland. Picture the warrior monk and the young king in those wild marshes – where no monastery was as yet built up, and where, upon that swamp, which was afterwards crowned with a splendid abbey, only a humble hut, and a rude cross of wood, were then to be seen.

The stormy old warrior Guthlac, who had done battle in many a hard-fought field, was at last weary of a soldier's life, and hearing that there was an island surrounded by a lake in a corner of Mercia, he got one of the local Lincolnshire fishermen to row him to the spot, where for some time he remained alone; here he was visited by Ethelbald, a man elegant in form, with a frame of iron, and a bold, undaunted spirit. There must have been some strange charm in the society of the soldier-monk, thus to have won over the young king to share with him such a solitude, for the marshes of Croyland must in those days have worn a most forbidding appearance, and even now, as they wave in summer, with their dark, coarse patches of goose-grass, and in some places, no stir of life is seen, excepting where the gosherd drives before him his noisy flock, an air of melancholy reigns over the scenery, and the mind unconsciously wanders back among the shadows of the dead.

Nor did Ethelbald, when he ascended the throne of Mercia, forget his exile, or his companion Guthlac, but gave the island of Croyland to the monks who had accompanied his friend, and preserved their piety amid all the privations which surrounded that solitude, and over the monument which the

Mercian king erected to the monk, was afterwards built the monastery of Croyland.

Ethelbald conquered Northumbria, and, aided by Cuthred, king of Wessex, obtained a victory over the Welsh; but although they had fought side by side, a spirit of jealousy nevertheless lurked within each bosom, and the Wessex king only waited for the first favourable opportunity to throw off the mask, and free himself from the power of the Mercian monarch.

Unforeseen circumstances, for some time, prevented Cuthred from openly taking the field against Ethelbald; his son rose up in rebellion, and no sooner was he put down, than one of his nobles, named Edelhun, took up arms, and would have conquered Cuthred, had he not been wounded at the very time when the battle had turned in his favour. These rebellions Ethelbald is accused of having fomented.

The rival kings at last met near Burford in Oxfordshire. Ethelbald had under his command the combined forces of Essex, Kent, East Anglia, and Mercia. Cuthred had the soldiers of Wessex alone, and the powerful arm of the former rebel, Edeldun, who was now his friend.

From Roger de Wendover, we have the following description of the battle, this being one of the most picturesque accounts from the pages of the early historians:

> "The attack on each side was headed by the standard-bearers of the opposing king; Edeldun bore the banner of Wessex, on which was emblazoned a golden dragon, and rushing forward with the ensign in his hand, he struck down the Mercian standard-bearer, a daring deed which called forth a loud shout from the army of Cuthred.
>
> A moment after, and the noise was drowned by the clashing of weapons, the mingled din, and roaring, and shouting, which swelled into the prolonged thunder of battle, amid which, if a brief pause intervened, it was filled up by the shrieks and groans of the wounded and

the dying, or the falling of some dreaded instrument which terminated the agony of death. Havoc spread like the destroying flames, into the midst of which the maddened masses plunged. Death and danger were disregarded; they fought as if the fate of a kingdom rested upon the blows dealt by each single arm.

For a moment the sunlight fell upon a mass of dazzling armour, gilding the plumed helmet, the pointed spear, the uplifted sword, and broad-edged battle-axe, and the rich banner, which, as it was borne onward amid the hurried charge, fluttered in gaudy colours, high over the heads of the eager combatants; a few moments more, and all this brave array was broken; another moving mass rushed onward in the thickest of the strife, the banner rocked and swayed, then went down; point after point the uplifted spears rose and sank, the helmets seemed as if crowded together; then the space which they occupied was filled up by others who passed onward; the moving waves heaved and fell, and passed along, while over all rolled that terrible sea of death which had swallowed up horse, rider, banner, sword, and battle-axe.

Foremost in the ranks stood Edeldun; wherever he moved, the spot was marked by the rapid circles which his ponderous battle-axe made around his head. At every stroke, death descended; wherever that terrible edge alighted, the hollow earth groaned, as it made room for another grave. No armour was proof against the blows which he dealt, for the fall of his arm was like that of a dreaded thunderbolt that rives asunder whatever it strikes.

Like two consuming fires, each having set in from opposite quarters and destroyed all that lay in their path, so did Edeldun and Ethelbald at last meet, flame hurrying to flame, nothing left between to consume. Behind each lay a dead, desolated, and blackened pathway."

Here we are compelled to halt; the sternest image we could gather from the pages of Homer would still leave the idea of their meeting imperfect. Ethelbald fled, having first exchanged a few blows with his dreaded adversary.

Wessex shook off the Mercian yoke, and Ethelbald never again raised his head so high as it had before been, when he looked proudly above those of the surrounding kings. Cuthred died, and the king of Mercia was soon after slain in a civil war in his own dominions. After his death, our attention is riveted upon the events which took place between these rival kingdoms, for the rest of the Saxon states, with scarcely an exception, were soon swallowed up in that great vortex – which at last bore the immortal name of England.

*

After the death of Cuthred, the throne of Wessex was occupied by Sigebyhrt, whose reign was brief and unpopular; he paid no regard to the laws which had been established by Ina; he took no heed of the remonstrances of his subjects, but when Cumbra, one of the most renowned of their nobles, boldly proclaimed the grievances of the people, he was put to death.

This was the signal for a revolt. The nobles assembled, the people were summoned to the council, and Sigebyhrt was deposed. Fearful of the vengeance of his subjects, the exiled king fled into the forest of Andredswold, where he concealed himself.

Here it is probable that for a time some peasants supplied him with food, and that the wild man of the wood was the talk and wonder of the neighbouring foresters.

One day, however, he was met by a swineherd named Ansiam, who had doubtless seen him beforetime when he visited his murdered master Cumbra – the swineherd knew him at first glance, and although he did not kill the king on the spot, yet he waited his time, and revenged his master's death by stabbing Sigebyhrt to the heart.

He appears to have watched him retire to his hiding-place, and when the fallen king lay stretched upon his couch of leaves, under the shade of gloomy and overhanging boughs, the savage swineherd stole silently through the thicket, and with one blow sent the unhappy sovereign to sleep his last sleep. As with the death of queen Ostrida, we find but a brief entry of his death in the old chronicles; he suited them not, was slain, cast aside, and so made room for another; and Cynewulf, in whose veins the blood of Woden was believed to flow, reigned in his stead.

*

We will now hasten on and make a brief survey of the state of Northumbria.

Ceolwulf, the patron of Bede, resigned his crown for the quiet of the cloister. Eadbert succeeded to the vacant throne. Whilst he was warring with the Picts, his dominions were invaded by the Mercians; he reigned for twenty-three years, then retired to a monastery, making the eighth Saxon king who had voluntarily laid aside the crown for the cowl. It is said that the fate of Sigebyrht and the fall of Ethelbald caused him to contrast their turbulent ending with the peaceful death-bed of Ceolwulf.

A strange change was thus wrought in the minds of these old Saxon kings – the glory of Woden had departed – no eager guests now rushed to the banquet halls of Valhalla; they looked for other glories beyond the grave.

Osulf succeeded his father to the throne of Northumbria, scarcely reigned a year, and was treacherously slain. Taking no warning by his fate, Edelwold was bold enough to accept the

crown; as usual, the path from the throne to the tomb was but a brief step, and he perished. Another and another still succeeded. Alred, a descendant of Ida, stepped into the empty seat, just looked around, and was driven out of the kingdom.

Then Ethelred came, put two of his generals to death on the evidence of two others, when, a few months after, the accusers turned round upon him, conquered him, and drove him from the throne. He fled like Alred.

Alfwold was the next king that came to be killed; he just reigned long enough to leave his name behind before he bade the world 'good night'. Osred next mounted, made his bow, was asked to sit down, then driven out.

Ethelred was beckoned back again. He came, stabbed Eardulf, who had aspired to the crown, and left him bleeding at the gate of a monastery; he dragged the children of Alfwold from York, and slaughtered them; and he put to death Osred, who, like himself, had been deposed, and just when he thought he had cleared away every obstacle, and was about to sit down upon the throne which he had stuffed with the dead to make it more easy, his subjects rewarded him for what he had done by slaying him.

He was followed by Osbald, who sat trembling with the crown upon his head for twenty-seven days, but not having reigned long enough to merit death, he was permitted to retire into a cloister.

Eardulf, whom we left bleeding at the gates of the monastery, was taken in and cured by the monks, fled to Rome, was received by Charlemagne, and at last placed upon the throne of Northumbria. His subjects soon revolted.

*

The crown and sceptre of Northumbria were then thrown aside – men shunned them as they would have done a plague; the curse of death was upon them, no man could take them up and live. 'Death kept his court' within the one, and when he wielded the other, the gold had ever pointed either to the grave or the cloister.

From such a murderous court, numbers of the nobles and bishops fled – the throne stood vacant for several years; no man was found bold enough to occupy it. The sword which ever hung there had fallen too often – not another Damocles could be found to ascend and survey the surrounding splendour from such a perilous position.

In looking over this long list of natural deaths, murders, and escapes which took place in one kingdom after the abdication of Eadbert, we have but recorded the events which occurred within forty short years, from 757 to about 790 A.D.

From the landing of Hengist and Horsa about three centuries before, nearly 150 kings had sat upon the different thrones of the Anglo-Saxon kingdoms. The bulk of these are unknown to us excepting by name; we can with difficulty just make out the petty states they reigned over, and that is nearly all.

Some died in the full belief of their heathen creed, with a firm faith that from a death-bed in the field of battle to the brutal immortality which their bloody deeds had merited was but a step, and that their happiness hereafter would consist of feasting and holiday murders in the halls of Woden.

Others calmly breathed their last with their dying eyes fixed upon the cross of Christ, while the anchor of their faith sunk noiselessly into the deep sea of death, and their weary barques were safely moored in that tranquil harbour where neither waves beat nor tempest roared, and where, at last, the 'storm-beat vessel safely rode'.

What a fearful history would those three centuries present if it could but be truly written – if we could see the everyday life of

those all but unknown kings! Their very graves are forgotten, their ashes scattered into dust, which ages ago mingled with the breeze, and was blown onward, unseen and unfelt.

Yet there was a time when even the meanest and the most unknown marched in pomp to the pagan temple, or lowly Christian church, when before them the noisy heralds went, and the applauding mob swelled behind, and rude as the crown and sceptre might be, and all the barbaric pearl and gold, still the holy oil was poured forth, and solemn prayers offered up, and the whole *witenagemot*, with the neighbouring nobles, were assembled together, and the little world around them for days after talked only of the coronation of the king.

Thousands at their command had mustered in battle, high nobles had bowed their heads before them; on a word from their

lips life or death frequently hung; valour and beauty were gathered around their thrones, and, when they rode forth in grand procession, the wondering crowd rushed out to gaze, even as it does now.

Edwin, with his banner borne before him, and Offa, with his trumpets sounding in the streets, were as much a marvel more than a thousand years ago, as any regent of our own time.

Yet there are many in the present day who think it a waste of time to dwell for a few hours upon the fates of those ancient kings, who, because they have been so long dead, are considered as undeserving of notice by those who seem to measure the events of the past by their own present insignificance; who, conscious that they themselves will be forgotten for ever as soon as the grave has closed over them, look begrudgingly upon almost every name that Time has not wholly obliterated.

16 OFFA THE TERRIBLE

> Come, come you spirits
> That tend on mortal thoughts, unsex me here;
> And fill me from the crown to the toe, top-full
> Of direst cruelty! make thick my blood,
> Stop up the access and passage to remorse,
> That no compunctious visitings of nature
> Shake my fell purpose, nor keep peace between
> The effect and it! Come to my woman's breasts,
> And take my milk for gall.
>
> – Shakspeare

To the kingdom of Mercia must we again turn the reader's attention for a few moments, and we take up the thread of our history from the death of Ethelbald, who, it will be remembered, fell while endeavouring to put down the rebellion which was headed by Bernred.

Of the latter we know nothing, excepting that he reigned for a few months, when he was either banished by the nobles, or driven from the throne by Offa, surnamed The Terrible, who descended from a brother of the king-slaying Penda. Though we have no clear proofs of the means by which Offa got possession of the crown of Mercia, there are many dark allusions scattered over the works of the clerical historians who were living during this period, which scarcely leave a doubt that he obtained the title of 'the Terrible' as a result of the violent measures he resorted to in attaining it. Bede says that he won the kingdom of Mercia "with a bloody sword."

One of the most romantic incidents which occur in the records of this period, is that which first introduced the future queen, Drida, into Offa's presence. She was a bold, beautiful, ambitious, and cruel woman, and appears to have been related to

Charlemagne. She committed some crime, for which she was doomed to undergo the ordeal of iron or fire; but although her deeds were so clearly proved, yet, as she was allied to Charlemagne, she was allowed the more merciful ordeal of water, and launched alone upon the pathless ocean, in a small boat, without either oar, rudder, or sail.

She was supplied with food for a few days, and left to the winds and waves, by which she was driven upon the British coast, somewhere on the territory over which Offa reigned. The storm-tossed beauty was conducted to the presence of the Mercian monarch, and having had ample time, while thrown from wave to wave, companionless upon the ocean, to concoct a colourful tale, she at once gave utterance to a story which won both the pity and the love of Offa. He assigned her to the care of his mother, where he frequently visited her, and then speedily married her.

> "He loved her for the dangers she had passed,
> And she loved him that he did pity them."

Such is the account given in his life, written by a monk of St Albans, the abbey of which was founded by Offa. If we could show that Homer was familiar to the cleric, we should be justified in imagining that he had transformed Ulysses into Drida, and changed Calypso to Offa; but whether or not, the wild legend has a doubtful look, though it has been quoted by many authors, and is included in various histories.

Offa was not a king who sat asleep with the sceptre in his hand; there was the wakeful and ambitious queen Drida now by his side; and, startling as it may seem, the dark events which stained their

reign, and the deeds of Offa's daughter, Edburga, would in the hands of a Shakespeare furnish the materials for a tragedy that might stand side by side with Macbeth.

Her cold cruel pride and chilling haughtiness are said to have broken the heart of Offa's mother, and, in a few months, to have hurried her into the grave. The blinded king saw only her superb beauty, for she appears to have been a female fiend that outwardly wore an angel's form.

Brave as a lion, and possessing talents that would have broken through the gloom of the most benighted period, the Mercian king marched onward from conquest to conquest, now achieving deeds that win our admiration, then sinking down to commit such crimes as must have made his subjects shudder.

On either side of him Drida and his daughter are ever rising up, like two spirits that attract our attention, as they come out in the sunshine to smile, or rush shrieking from the darkness into which they had plunged, to accomplish some new and horrible deed.

They seem to come and go with a terrible distinctness that makes us tremble as they either approach or vanish, as if Mercy fled before them, and we heard, in the place from which she had hurried affrighted, dying moans, and Love wailing upon the very lips on which he, expiring, kissed the poison of death.

All is as dim as a dream, or as startling as some appalling reality which we look upon with a doubtful consciousness. So perplexing and unnatural appear the events of this period that the majority of historians seem to have paused, looked round for a moment in doubt and wonder, and then hastened off to visit less forbidding scenes, as if they feared to grapple with the shadows and the realities that here seem to be always exchanging places – throwing aside what is only doubtful as feeble, and dreading to look among events which seem cruel and unnatural for their horrible truth, as if years, because they have rolled away, were empty of events, and days dawned not upon hopes and fears as in the present day.

Wild roses blew, and nightingales sang, as they do now, and the smell and sound were as sweet to those who went out to look and listen, in the noonday or in the twilight, and returning, were stabbed by the way, or laid their heads upon their pillows unconscious of the poison that would, before the dawning, with a noiseless power, unlock and throw open the silent gates of death. The murdered kings who were hurried into their graves by these merciless women, once enjoyed the tender green of Spring, and the sober gold of the Autumnal foliage, as we still do.

What a period are we now picturing! A king is murdered and consigned to his grave; his successor builds a monastery, or makes a pilgrimage to Rome, and believes that he has purchased forgiveness. A queen rushes out of the chamber, and leaves behind her the yet warm body of the husband she has poisoned; she crosses the sea and becomes an abbess. A young king comes wooing, in all the hey-day of life, is allured from the banquet by the mother of the fair princess for whose hand he is suing, taken into the next apartment, and put to death.

And these are the solemn truths of English history – the dark deeds that were done by those who sat on the very throne which Alfred the Great himself occupied. The events which we record in this chapter were written down by Alfred nearly a thousand years ago; he heard them from the lips of those whose fathers had lived and moved through all these stirring scenes.

We have already shown in what a defenceless state Northumbria was left. Offa, doubtless well acquainted with the civil dissent by which it was rent asunder, attacked it, as his uncle Penda had done beforetime. What advantages he gained, are not recorded.

He next marched into Kent, fought a hardly contested battle at Otunford or Otford, conquered, and annexed that kingdom to Mercia. At the battle of Bensington, he defeated Cynewulf, king of Wessex, and either took

possession of his dominions, or compelled him to become his ally; that Offa did not dethrone him is evident from an incident which we shall shortly have to narrate.

The ancient Britons were not yet at rest, for whenever a favourable opportunity occurred, they sallied forth from the corners into which they were driven, slew and plundered the Saxons, and hastened back again into their mountain fortresses as soon as they saw a stronger force approaching. They had several times invaded Mercia, and, emboldened by their success, at length drove the Saxons who dwelt beside the Severn further into the heart of the kingdom.

Offa at last armed and led a powerful force against them. The Welsh fled into their hidden fastnesses, where they stood until his back was turned upon them, when they again ventured forth. The Mercian king once more approached, when the Welsh as usual fled, and all the open country from the Severn to the river Wye was cleared of them; this time Offa determined to imprison this daring remnant of the old Cymry within their own limited territories.

To accomplish this, he commanded a vast trench to be dug, and a huge rampart to be thrown up, as the Roman generals had done centuries before; and this gigantic work he extended for nearly a hundred miles, carrying it overland, from the river Dee to the entrance of the Wye, strengthening it also with fortresses, which he manned with chosen and hardy soldiers.

But the Welsh were not long before they filled up a large portion of the ditch, made a wide gap through the ramparts, and fell upon Offa's warriors while they were holding their Christmas feast, and more than one Saxon fortress was left standing all throughout that dark winter night without a sentinel.

Offa again arose, and avenged the deaths of his followers. The king of North Wales and many of the old British nobles fell at the battle of Rhuddlan, and those who were taken prisoner were doomed to the severest slavery. Mercia was not disturbed again by the Welsh during the reign of Offa the Terrible.

The remains of the immense work, which ages after retained the name of Claudh Offa, or Offa's Dyke, are still visible, and for centuries were the acknowledged barrier that divided England from Wales. Many an unrecorded combat was fought on those ancient boundaries, and the remains of many a hero, whose name will never now be known, lie buried deep down within those filled-up trenches.

Perhaps Offa's marriage with Drida was the first cause of his opening a correspondence with the renowned Charlemagne; but whatever it might be, the letters that passed between them reveal the earliest traces of a protected trade with the continent. The Frankish king offered to permit all pilgrims to pass securely through his dominions; and such as came not on religious missions, but were engaged in commerce, were to pass safely to and fro, after paying the requisite duties.

To Offa, Charlemagne sent as proofs of his kindness and friendship a rich belt, an Hungarian sword, and two cloaks of silk. Trifling as these matters may at first appear, they show what silent strides civilization was already making; duties paid on commerce for protection are different things to the dogs and horses which, centuries before, the Britons were wont to present to the Roman emperors whenever they required their aid.

Egbert, who was destined to become the grandfather of Alfred the Great, resided for a time at Offa's court; but when Brihtric ascended the throne of Wessex, and demanded the hand of Edburga, Egbert hastened to France, where he became a great favourite with Charlemagne. There he not only improved himself in learning and military tactics, but by departing from Britain he saved his life, for Brihtric was already jealous of the fame he had won while residing with Offa, and sought to destroy him.

Had the gifted young prince offended Edburga by refusing her hand, and was this jealousy aroused by queen Drida and her daughter? There is one of those mysterious blanks here which we are at a loss to fill up adequately, for it is not clear that Egbert fled to Offa for protection, but on the contrary he appears to have been a guest of the Mercian king for some time before Brihtric sought the hand of Edburga.

According to William of Malmesbury, Egbert's claim to the throne of Wessex was superior to Brihtric's – but we must not pass over the event by which the throne of Wessex became vacant. Cynewulf we have already seen measuring arms with Offa at the battle of Bensington, where he was defeated.

He became jealous of Cyneheard, who was a brother of Sigebyrht, a king who had been driven from the throne of Wessex, and he either sought to slay him, or banish him from the kingdom. Cyneheard made his escape, but no further than into a neighbouring wood, near Merton in Surrey, where he lay concealed, having, however, a number of spies about him, who were on the lookout for the king; for Cyneheard had resolved to strike the first blow; nor was it long before an opportunity arose.

A woman lived at Merton, whom Cynewulf frequently visited, often coming with only a few attendants; his enemy was on the look out, and soon surrounded the house after he had seen the king enter.

Cynewulf threw open the door, rushed out, and wounded Cyneheard; a dozen swords were at once uplifted against him; the king of Wessex fought alone against them all; his followers were in another part of the house; there was not one nearby to aid him, and he was slain.

Assistance came too late; the tumult had aroused those within, and, snatching up their weapons, they hastened out to defend their master; they found him fallen and bleeding beside the threshold.

Cyneheard parleyed with them for a few moments; he offered them lands and rich rewards if they would serve him. They refused his offer with disdain, and foot to foot, and hand to hand, they fought until only one remained alive; the dead followers and their dead king lay side by side.

The news of Cynewulf's death soon spread, and others speedily rode up to avenge the murder of their sovereign. To these Cyneheard made the same offers, and received the same reply, their only answer being the naked weapons they presented; they had come to avenge the death of their king, to demand life for life, and they fell upon Cyneheard and his followers and slew them all, excepting one, who was severely wounded. Thus Brihtric ascended the throne of Wessex, and married the daughter of Offa – and dark was the bridal chamber into which he entered.

*

We turn to another scene. A young lady was leaning upon the ledge of the palace window, watching a long train of knights entering the court yard, and admiring the beauty of one who appeared to be their chief, when she called upon her mother to come forward and witness the scene.

That lady was the youngest daughter of Offa. The woman she called her mother was Queen Drida, and the youth she had admired, Ethelbert, had just succeeded to the throne of East Anglia, and had now come with costly presents, to seek her hand and form an alliance with the powerful house of Mercia.

Queen Drida had those beyond the sea whom she wished to serve, with whom she had in vain endeavoured to unite her daughter in marriage; there was but one left single now – the youngest, Alfleda, and the youthful king of East Anglia had come to carry her off also. She had seen her husband welcome him, and the warm reception Ethelbert had received was as gall and wormwood to her. The evil spirit rose strong within her, and she resolved he should never again quit her roof until he was carried to his grave.

She called Offa aside. She well knew the power of her beauty; and the weak point of her husband – ambition. She pointed out the number of followers who, encamped outside the palace walls, had accompanied Ethelbert. She assured him that marriage was not the errand he had come upon; that his design extended to gaining the crown of Mercia.

Offa doubted her assertions. Cunning as she was cruel, she turned round the point of her argument, then proceeded to show him that if even the young king did marry their daughter, he would, from the moment of his union, consider himself to be the heir to the throne of Mercia, and he would hourly look for Offa's death; nay, he would seek to hasten it if an opportunity offered.

She showed him how Ethelbert had made himself acquainted with the roads which led through Mercia – how he must have observed every salient point of the kingdom as he passed along; and, perceiving that the king looked perplexed, she added: "Either he will shortly be the cause of your death, or you must now be the cause of his."

The poor blinded husband admitted the truth of her argument, and confessed that he was exposed to peril; yet, according to one of the old chroniclers, he turned away, and firmly refused to partake in such a detestable crime as she suggested – which, he added, "would bring eternal disgrace upon me and my successors."

The two kings sat down to the feast. The hall of the palace resounded with mirth. Drida came in every now and then, and when called upon to account for her absence, said she had been looking after the apartment which she was fitting up for the reception of her royal guest; for Ethelbert had spent the previous night in his camp, as the day was drawing to a decline long before he reached the royal residence.

In the room which the queen had set apart for the East Anglian king, she had caused a splendid throne to be erected, which was overhung with curious drapery, and surmounted by a rich canopy. In the adjoining apartment a beautiful couch was fitted up, on which he was to sleep.

She came in again with the same smiling look, and armed with that beauty which Time had only rendered more imposing and majestic. She sat down to the feast, and whiled away the hours with pleasant and playful conversation. All looked calm, and cheerful, and captivating, while behind the scenes, there was planned dark and deep-moving murder, and savage vengeance; and all the awful turmoil which ever beats about the restless brain of disappointed ambition.

The Saxon gleemen sung and tumbled; the wine-cup circulated – rich brew sweetened with honey and flavoured with spices was handed round in costly vessels; mead mellowed with the juice of mulberries and strong wines made odoriferous with the flowers and sweet-herbs passed from hand to hand; and all went 'merry as a marriage bell'

And then the siren turned sweetly round, and assumed one of those studied looks which had saved her from the fiery ordeal – which, when tossed like a wave upon the ocean, had won its way through Offa's heart to his throne; and she exclaimed (and probably laid her hand upon the shoulder of her unsuspecting victim, as she spoke;) "Come, my son, Alfleda anxiously awaits you in the chamber I have prepared; she wishes to hear the words of love which her intended husband has to say."

It is not improbable that she led him in playfully by the hand – and not one of his attendants followed. When he entered the room, she bade him sit down upon the throne which stood in readiness to receive him; and, looking round with feigned wonder, pretended confision; why had her daughter not already arrived?

With the merry mead playing about his brain, we can almost picture Ethelbert uttering some jest as he threw himself laughing into the gorgeous seat. We can see the last smile linger about Drida's eye, the sparkling fire of vengeance heaving up, as the demon-like glare flashed forth, the instant she had released her hand – for the moment Ethelbert threw himself upon the throne, it sunk beneath him, into the pit over which it had been placed.

There was help at hand, concealed men, who listened silently for the fall. They rushed forth, with Drida aiding them. Beds, pillows, and hangings were all thrown upon the shrieking king, to drown his cries; and when all was silent, the trap-door was closed.

There is scarcely a doubt that Offa was privy to the deed. The fact of his taking possession of East Anglia immediately after the murder of Ethelbert is a strong proof of his guilt; though some have attempted to show that he but seized upon it in self-defence, when the East Anglians swore to revenge the death of their sovereign.

Alfleda, the fair betrothed, fled from the murderous court to the monastery of Croyland; and in the midst of those wild marshes, where the bittern boomed and the tufted plover went ever wailing through the air, she assumed the habit of a nun, and dedicated the remainder of her days, which were few, to the service of God.

In the *Life of Offa*, which we have before alluded to, it is stated that the Mercian monarch banished the royal murderess to one of the most solitary fortresses in his dominions – and that she carried with her an immense treasure which she had reaped from many a crime, and wrung from the many who had groaned beneath her oppression. Lonely and neglected, she was left to gloat over the gold for which she had imperilled her soul.

But vengeance was not long before it overtook her. The lonely fortress to which she was banished was attacked by robbers, her treasures taken from her, and she herself cruelly tortured then thrown into a well, where she was left to expire, unmourned and unpitied. Her end bears a strange resemblance to that of the youthful king whom she caused to be so ruthlessly butchered.

*

Edburga inherited all her mother's vices; she was envious, ambitious, and cruel. Those who became favourites with her husband, Brihtric, she hated, allowing no one to share his confidence or his counsel without drawing down her vengeance; and when she could not succeed in obtaining their disgrace or banishment, she caused them to be secretly poisoned, for there were ever emissaries at her elbow, ready to do their wicked work.

Like her mother Drida, she found a pleasure in the execution of dark and dreadful deeds. There was a youth who stood high in the estimation of the king, whom Edburga had long endeavoured – but in vain – to overthrow. Brihtric turned a deaf ear to all her complaints, and seldom trusted his envied favourite out of his sight.

But she had sent too many of her victims to the grave, and was acquainted with too many ready roads, which led directly to death, to abandon her prey; so, following her old sure and speedy path, she poured poison into his wine-cup. That night the king drank out of the same vessel as his favourite, and died. And so she sent one soul more to the dark dominions than she had intended.

Dreading the vengeance of her nobles, she packed up all the treasures she could find in the palace and hastened off to France. The West Saxons passed a decree that no king's consort should in future share her husband's throne, and that the title of queen should be abolished.

The murderess presented herself with all her treasures before Charlemagne, and, doubtless, as her mother Drida had beforetime done, when tossed by the angry ocean upon the British coast, she feigned some story to account for her coming. Charlemagne asked her whether she would choose himself or his son, who stood beside him, to be her husband.

She boldly replied "Your son, because he is the youngest."

The monarch answered that if she had chosen him, it had been his intention to have given her to his son; but now, he added, "you shall have neither". This was a strong proof that she had concocted some tale about the death of Brihtric, for such a proposition would never have been made to her had Charlemagne known that she had just hurried, with breathless haste, from the dead body of her murdered husband.

She entered a monastery, became abbess, but was quickly driven out because of the immoral and infamous life she led there.

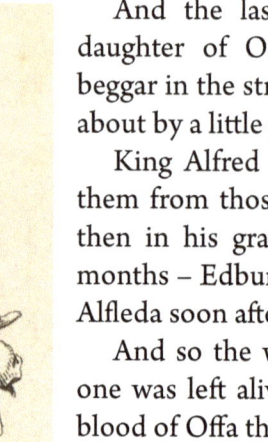

And the last scene of all – the haughty daughter of Offa finally became a common beggar in the streets of Pavia, where she was led about by a little girl.

King Alfred mentions these facts; he heard them from those who knew her well. Offa was then in his grave. His son reigned but a few months – Edburga died a beggar in the streets – Alfleda soon after in the monastery of Croyland.

And so the whole line was swept away; not one was left alive in whose veins there ran the blood of Offa the Terrible. Neither sable tragedy nor dark romance were ever woven from wilder materials than the historical truths which form this gloomy chapter.

17 EGBERT, KING OF ALL THE SAXONS

"O my poor kingdom, sick with civil blows!
When that my care could not withhold thy riots,
What wilt thou do, when riot is thy care?
O, thou wilt be a wilderness again,
Peopled with wolves, thy old inhabitants!"

– Shakespeare

Egbert was no sooner informed of the death of Brihtric, than he hastened out of France, to take possession of the throne of Wessex, and never had a Saxon sovereign that had hitherto swayed the perilous sceptre come armed with the experience of this new king.

He had studied in the stern school of Charlemagne, had studied the policies pursued by that great monarch, both in the council and in the camp, and was well prepared to collect and reduce to order the stormy elements which had so long been let loose over Britain; for, in addition to the civil discords which shook the land, the Danes had already invaded our island.

Few kings had ever received a warmer welcome from their subjects than that which awaited Egbert on his accession, for he was the last descendant of the race of Cerdric.

Kent, Essex, and East Anglia had already acknowledged the power of Mercia; Northumbria had long been rent asunder by internal dissensions; and Sussex was by this time united to Wessex.

Having thus doubled its strength and enlarged its territories, the kingdom over which Egbert reigned was, with the exception of Mercia, the only independent state that stood unbroken amid the ruins of the Octarchy.

Kenwulf sat firmly upon the Mercian throne, whose foundation Offa had so well consolidated. Egbert watched him with an eagle eye, but though ever on the alert, the Mercian king was too wary to become an aggressor; and the Wessex sovereign knew too well the strength of his rival, to be the first to commence an attack.

Both kingdoms seemed overhung with the same threatening sky, but no one could tell on which it would first break, though all could foresee that, in spite of its remaining so long stationary, the storm must at eventually burst. As the petty states around them crumbled to pieces, and were gathered up and built in upon other foundations, so did each silently seek to possess himself of the ruins and outdo the other, making an outward parade of their strength – yet each tacitly acknowledged, by their forbearance, how much they envied, yet respected, their neighbour's power.

Like two expert wrestlers, each retained his hold, without venturing to overthrow his adversary. This state of things could not last long; yet while Kenwulf lived, he kept the balance so equally poised, that, with all his ambition, Egbert ventured not to touch the scale.

Then the king of Mercia died, and, from that moment, Wessex slowly gained the ascendancy. Until now Egbert had been content with carrying his arms into Cornwall and Devonshire, and waging war with the Britons. After Kenwulf's death, however, he aimed at the sole sovereignty of Britain, and circumstances soon favoured his long-meditated conquest. Had Egbert died first, Kenwulf would have aspired to the same power.

The Mercian king left his son Kinelm, who was only seven years of age, and heir to the throne, to the charge of his sisters. Windreda, the eldest, was not long before she caused her brother to be put to death.

His tutor, Askebert, was the instrument chosen by this unnatural sister to accomplish the deed. It is said that she promised to share with him the sovereignty. Under the pretence of hunting, the innocent prince was led into a neighbouring wood, and there he was murdered. The spot in which the body was interred was, after some time, discovered by a herdsman, who went in search of one of his cows which had gone astray; a miracle in the old monkish legends is appended to the discovery.

The sceptre of Mercia was then wrested from the hands of Windreda by her uncle, Ceolwulf, who, however, did not retain it long before he himself was driven from the throne by Beornwulf, in a revolution which shook the kingdom of Mercia to its core.

Egbert still stood aloof from all this; the time for action had not yet arrived. He foresaw that the last usurper would not long remain inactive; and he was right.

Beornwulf soon rushed headlong into a war with Wessex. The battle took place at Wilton, which, in ancient times was called Ellan. Although the Mercians mustered together the largest force upon the field, Egbert, after a sharp contest, won the victory.

Although the king of Wessex did not carry his victorious arms at once into Mercia, he lost no time in annexing Kent to his dominions, thus weakening at once his rival's power. To accomplish this, he despatched his son Ethelwulf, the father of our Alfred the Great, with a strong force into Kent, and the vassal king was driven across the Thames.

Egbert next promised to support the East Anglians if they would rise and declare themselves independent of the Mercian king. He kept his word. Beornwulf fell in the first battle.

Ludecan succeeded him, and also perished in the next contest.

Wiglaf then took the command of the Mercian forces, but before he had time to strengthen his army, and make up for their previous defeats, Egbert was upon him, and the power of Wessex was at last triumphant.

Wiglaf fled into the monastery of Croyland, and appears to have been so closely pursued that he was compelled to seek shelter in the very cell which the daughter of Offa occupied – the sanctity of which the invaders respected. Here he remained for four months.

What a shock must the feelings of the fair nun have undergone when the last defender of Mercia rushed into her little apartment to save his life. From the very night when she fled from her father's palace, pale and woe-begone, and horror-struck at the murder of her intended husband – from that very night had the fortune of her family begun to decline, and now she was all that remained of the once powerful house of Offa. What changes had that Saxon princess witnessed, what shifting scenes could she recall as she sat in the solitude of her cell, contemplating the past as it rose before her!

By the intercession of Siward, Wiglaf was permitted to occupy the throne of Mercia, on condition that he paid tribute to Egbert. The abbot of Croyland attested the payment.

Prior to this period, the Northumbrians grew weary of being without a king, and Eanred now sat upon the throne. During the reign of Kenwulf, he had been bold enough to invade Mercia.

As Egbert had by this time subdued the whole Octarchy, with the exception of Northumbria, he decided to carry his victorious army into Deiri and Bernicia.

Eanred well knew that it was useless to measure arms with a monarch who had already compelled five Saxon kingdoms to acknowledge his power, so he came forth submissively, and, like the rest, became a tributary vassal to the king of Wessex.

Egbert next invaded Wales, and penetrated into the very heart of Snowdon: victory still attended him. From the Tweed to the Land's End of Cornwall, no one now arose to dispute his sovereign sway. No Saxon king had ever before ruled over such a vast extent of territory, for he was at last the sole king of all England, although he never assumed that proud title. Neither did any Saxon king after him ever rule over such a length and breadth of land.

*

We have before stated that, during the reign of Offa, the Danes had landed in England.

They first arrived with three ships, then approached one of the royal cities. The sheriff of the place, thinking they were foreign merchants, rode up with a few attendants to inquire their business. Their answers being unsatisfactory, he ordered them to be driven away; they fell upon him, and he, with all who accompanied him, were slain.

The Danes then plundered the town; but before they escaped to their ships, Offa's soldiers attacked them.

After this defeat, they returned again, landed in Northumbria, ravaged the country, sacked the abbey of Lindisfarne, slew several of the monks, then retreated with an immense spoil to their ships. At several other parts of the island they had also landed, all prior to Egbert taking the throne of Wessex.

In the year 832, they came again. By now, Egbert had made the whole kingdom of the Octarchy bow before the power of Wessex, and perhaps had sat down, expecting to spend the remainder of his days peaceably upon his throne; but tidings came that a number of

these savage pagans had landed on the Isle of Sheppey, slaughtered several of the inhabitants, and, laden with plunder, had again escaped to sea without a single vessel pursuing them.

The next year, the Danes came with 35 ships, and were met by Egbert at Charmouth, in Dorsetshire, and if the English were not defeated in this engagement, they lost a considerable number of men, amongst whom were two bishops and two ealdermen; while the Danes sustained but little loss, and escaped, as before, with their ships.

So serious had the ravages of the Vikings now become that a council was held in London, to devise the best means to prevent their depredations. At this council Egbert presided, and, according to the charter which Wiglaf granted to the abbey of Croyland, wherein direct allusion is made to a promise given at the time, there were present King Egbert and Athelwulf his son, and all the bishops and great ealdermen of England, all consulting together as to the best means of repelling the constant incursions of the Danes on the English coast.

These northern invaders soon found ready allies amongst the remnant of the ancient Cymry, who still inhabited a corner of Cornwall and the adjacent neighbourhood. The Cymry were as ready as in the days of King Arthur to ally themselves with any enemy who was bold enough to attack the Saxons. But the martial spirit of the ancient Britons had all but died out; the few embers that remained, when stirred, retained all their former glow, then faded again to ashy grey, and sank into a lesser compass at every touch; for the smouldering waste had slowly gone on, year after year, and no new fuel having been added, the hidden sparks huddled hopelessly together. Liberty had neglected to come, as the bards had promised she would do: the altar and the spark were still there, but the long-looked for salvation never came, which was to light the whole island with its blaze.

Still, the old Cymry were not yet dead; they hailed the Danes as their deliverers, and thinly as they were sprinkled over the surrounding country, they gladly mustered what force they could, and joined the Vikings at Hengston Hill, in Cornwall. Egbert met them with a well-appointed army, and defeated their united forces with terrible slaughter.

The following year, Egbert died, after a reign of 37 years, and was succeeded by his son, Ethelwulf, the father of Alfred the Great. The king of all the Saxons had gone to his grave with the fond hope that the whole Octarchy had now become united as one family, all acknowledging one sway; that the civil dissensions by which each separate state had so long been torn asunder had for ever ceased. And as the Danish invaders had not again appeared since their dreadful defeat at Hengston Hill, he closed his dying eyes, and left his country at peace.

But scarcely was he within his grave before the northern hordes again poured into England, spreading greater consternation than the Saxons had ever done amongst the Britons. The hour of retribution, which the Cymry had so long looked for, was fast approaching, but few of their ancient race lived to witness its fulfilment; for time, and conquest, and slavery, and death, had left but few of those early inhabitants behind, whose forefathers first landed upon our island, and called it the Country of Sea Cliffs.

And now we have reached another of those ancient landmarks, which stand wide apart along the shores of History, the grey monuments which overlook that still sea of Death, where nameless millions have for ages been buried. From these we must now turn our gaze upon another race, more savage and uncivilized than the preceding invaders ever were, when, nearly four centuries before, they first rowed their long chiules over the same stormy seas, and marvelled to find an island in the ocean, which contained walled cities and stately temples, and tall columns, that might have vied with classical Rome.

In the next volume, it is to the Danes that we will turn – those children of the creeks, who, under the guidance of their sea kings, followed the road of the swans, as they called the ocean, and hewed out a home with their swords, wherever the winds or the waves wafted or drifted them.

APPENDICES

ANGLO-SAXON RELIGION

We have already described the paganism of the Saxons, both as it existed on the Continent, and after their arrival in England; and we must now consider their conversion to Christianity, and the early modes of worship which they adopted.

When they landed in England, they found that among the Britons, Christianity had become established, and had overpowered and supplanted the remains of the druidism which been the original religion of the Britons. The idolatry that existed had assumed a more classic form; and instead of the grim wicker idols of the druids, the more sightly forms of the heathen gods, which the Romans worshipped, had usurped their places.

Among the ancient Cymry (or Welsh) who had not come into such close contact with the Roman conquerors, the old druidic forms of idolatry still lingered; though through them we are enabled to catch faint glimpses of the Deity, and to discover a slow, but sure approach towards the Creator.

We have already shown how the Saxon invasion checked the progress of Christianity – how the churches were overthrown, and the priests massacred, until pope Gregory sent over Augustine, who succeeded in converting the Saxon king, Ethelbert, to the religion of Christ.

We saw how Paulinus accompanied Edilburga into Northumbria, and Edwin, the king of the Deira and Bernicia, became a convert to the holy faith. We have shown how the abbey of Croyland rose up amid the wild marshes of Lincolnshire, and the gospel sound was carried through the vast territory of Mercia, until at last the whole of the Saxon Octarchy bowed before the image of the dying Redeemer.

To the forms of worship which were adopted in these ancient Christian churches, we must now turn.

*

A rude wooden cross, planted by the roadside, a humble cell scooped out of the rock, or a wattled shed, thatched with the tufted rushes or the broad-leaved water-flags, first marked the places of worship of the primitive Christians. Some who had come over settled down upon waste and lonely places; their piety and peaceful habits soon attracted the attention of the neighbouring peasantry, and of the chiefs, who granted them permission to reside and build upon the soil; allowed them to fell timber in the adjacent forest, or to hew stone from the distant quarry.

Nor were they long in procuring assistance; many more came and laboured for the love of God; they dug foundations; they mixed cement; the trees were sawn, and squared into beams; a forge was erected, and, as the blue smoke curled above the landscape, the clattering of the brawny smith was heard upon the anvil, as he shaped the iron which bound together beam and rafter. At length a tower rose up above the wild waste of marshes, and

in the morning, and the evening, and often at intervals during the day, the bell was heard to toll; and as the sound fell upon the wayfarer's ears who journeyed past, he thought of life, and death, and heaven.

Larger estates were given to them; they received donations, houses, and lands, and forests, which were secured by grants and charters, and attested by the signatures of kings. These bequests were made from both love and fear, in the hope of escaping future punishments, and through the intercession of the priests to enter heaven.

Thus was a door thrown open, through which both good and evil were admitted. The truly pious and the hardened sinner alike received encouragement. Bells were rung, and masses said, no matter for whom, as long as the altar was piled high with treasure – and mankind was taught that forgiveness could be purchased by wealth.

Still the knee had to be bent, and prayers offered up, penances performed, and fastings endured, before the conscientious priest promised to intercede for the sinner. Then the wooden cross, the naked walls, and the floor strewn with rushes were replaced by woven tapestry and glaring pictures, by graven images and relics of saints, by costly vessels of gold and silver, rich vestments and dazzling gems, and by all the glitter and pomp which had hitherto been confined to courts, or borne in triumphal processions – they were all called up to decorate the buildings dedicated to God.

In place of the lowly dwelling, mighty constructions were erected by skilful architects, whose roofs seemed to rest on the rim of the horizon, and the traveller looked in vain for those beautiful openings in the landscape which had so long been familiar to his eye. Mighty barons, who had distinguished themselves in many a hard-fought field, became abbots; kings laid aside their costly robes, their crowns, and sceptres, put on the grey homely serge of the pilgrim, and, with staff in hand, journeyed weary miles to kneel before the shrines of saints, and either left their bones to moulder in a foreign land, or returned home again to die in the quiet solitude of the cloister – leaving miles of hill and vale, and wood and river, to enrich the revenues of the grey abbey in which they expired, amid the shady sadness of long-embowered aisles.

These religious houses were happy havens for the poor and needy, the hungry, the wretched, and the oppressed. They became landmarks to the sick, storm-tossed, and rain-drenched wayfarer. All who were sheltered and relieved; none were sent away empty-handed, for spiritual and bodily comfort were alike administered to all. They were the only resting places where the traveller could halt, and find refreshment and welcome, where his steed was stabled, his wants attended to, and where, without charge, he was dismissed on the morrow with a prayer and a blessing.

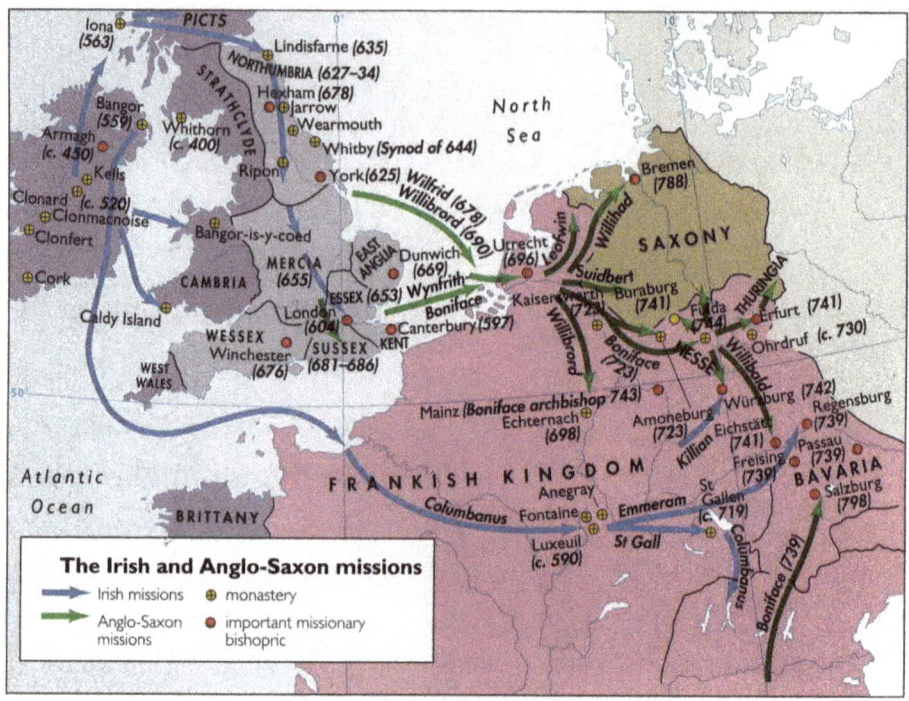

Nor did their works of charity end here: they sent out missionaries to other countries, to the benighted land from which their ancestors first came.

Although there were many things in their ancient forms of worship which in us awaken a sigh or a smile, we must remember that religion was then in its infancy – that they had but few guides, and only few books to instruct them. There were only a few able to translate the gospels from the Latin into the Saxon tongue; such versions as they were able to make were crude and incorrect, and many of the priests were unable to instruct them in points of faith. They ventured little further in their instruction than to teach that the soul was immortal, and lived in a future state, where the good were rewarded, and the evil punished; that Christ died for our salvation – that the dead arose, and the faithful and just would at last be admitted into eternal glory.

Into the more intricate mysteries of our religion, they did not venture. Every priest was commanded to read the gospels, and to study the Bible so that he might teach the people. Several valuable manuscipts of the translation of the gospel into the Saxon language, which were written between the reigns of Alfred and Harold, are still in existence.

Although they used the cross as the sign of their salvation, they were taught not to reverence the wood, but to bear in mind the form of he who had suffered upon it. They held relics in high veneration; and though the remains of good and holy men cannot be contemplated without awakening a religious feeling, they carried their reverence to a superstitious excess; they believed that the greatest miracles could be worked through relics, and that they were the only safeguards against disease, magic, and witchcraft.

The priests were only allowed to celebrate mass when fasting; nor, unless in cases of sickness, was this ceremony to be held anywhere but upon the altar in the church; and to this altar no woman was permitted to approach during its celebration; neither dogs nor swine were allowed to come within the enclosure that surrounded the holy edifice. The purest of bread, wine, and water, were only to be used in celebrating the Eucharist, and the sacramental cup was to be formed of gold, or silver, glass, or tin; and none made of earth or wood were permitted to be used.

The altar was always to be kept clean, and covered; and the priest was to have his missal, his psalter, his reading-book, penitential, numeral, hand-book, and singing-book. He was also to learn some handicraft, and to abolish all witchcraft.

Each priest performed his own allotted duty; the ostiary guarded the church doors and tolled the bell; the exorcist drove out devils, and sprinkled houses which were infested with witches and foul fiends, with abyssum; the lector read the gospels to the  congregation; the acolyth held the tapers while the lector read; the deacon attended on the mass-priest, placed the oblations on the altar, baptized children, and administered the Eucharist to the

people; the sub-deacon had charge of the holy vessels, and waited at the altar while the mass-priest preached and consecrated the Eucharist.

The bishop was looked up to as a comforter to the wretched, and a father to the poor; the priests were forbidden to carry their controversies before a lay tribunal, and when they could not settle it amongst themselves, it was left to the decision of the bishop. The high-born were taught not to despise those that were lowly; they were ordered to teach youth with care – to give alms, and chant holy hymns during the distribution; to humble themselves, and to become examples of mildheartedness.

Many of the penances they inflicted were severe. He who was guilty of any heinous offence was to lay aside his weapons, travel barefoot for many weary miles, and could not seek household shelter during the night. He was to pay no regard to his dress, nor to enter a bath, neither might he eat flesh, nor taste strong drink, but instead had to fast, watch, and pray, both by day and night.

The wealthy, however, could evade the heaviest penances by giving alms; the following extract will show to what useful purposes the church applied these penalties:

"He that hath ability may raise a church to the praise of
God, and if he has wherewithal, let him give land to it,
and allow ten young men, so that they may serve in it,
and minister the daily service.

He may repair churches where he can, and make folk-
ways, with bridges over deep waters, and over miry
places; assist poor men's widows, step-children, and foreigners.

He may free his own slaves, and redeem the liberty of
those who belong to other masters, and especially the
poor captives of war. He may feed the needy, house
them, clothe and warm them, and give them baths and beds."

Thus did our pious ancestors make crime administer to the wants of the poor; they filtered the pure waters of charity from these corrupt sources, and displayed a wisdom which our modern legislators have yet to be taught.

ANGLO-SAXON GOVERNMENT AND LAW

When the Saxons first landed in England, they could have had no knowledge of the Roman laws which were then in existence there; for the government of the Roman conquerors had long replaced the primitive customs which had been used by the ancient Britons before the landing of Julius Cæsar.

We have already shown that the earliest of the Saxon invaders were led by a chief who claimed his descent from Odin, and was acknowledged as leader by the consent of his followers; and so he was also allowed the largest share of the plunder or captives which were taken in war.

Thus it would naturally follow that when they came to settle down upon the soil which they had conquered, the power of the chief would be acknowledged; and to him would be given the greatest part of the land, while amongst his followers such shares would be distributed as were considered proportionate to their rank.

After having conquered and divided the land, they would naturally unite together to defend the possessions they had won, and the chief, or his descendant, – if found worthy of being still retained at their head, by his wisdom or valour – would, either in peace or war, continue to hold the title and power of ruler; and thus would governments be formed, thrones established, and laws made by the wealthy and powerful, to keep their followers and captives in subjection.

Nor would it be inevitable that in all instances would the conquered be made captives. Many, by their valour and opposition, would still present a formidable front to the invaders;

and as both parties would in time grow weary of a continued system of attack or defence, concessions would be made, peace agreed upon, the land divided, vows sworn, and penalties fixed, to be paid by those who first broke the treaty.

In such cases, war would not be entered into by either party without their first stating the grievances. This, again, would lead to discussions, assemblies, accusations and defences; times and places would be allotted for meeting; and so courts and tribunals were formed; and thus in all countries did the development of law and civilization commence.

We have shown how England was at first divided into separate kingdoms; how chief after chief came over, fought, conquered, and established a separate state, until the Octarchy was formed; and that when the whole island was occupied, the Saxon kings began to make war upon each other, until state after state was subdued, and one king at last reigned over all.

Governors were placed over different divisions of this vast extent of territory; and these, again, placed officers over the sub-divisions: thus there were earls or aldermen, sheriffs, or shrieves, officers to each hundred or tithing; headboroughs, frankpledges, who attended the court-leet which was held at given periods, and accounted for all grievances or violations of the law.

The first laws made would naturally be those which protected persons and property, to punish acts of violence and theft, and to prevent personal vengeance being inflicted. Thus, murder might be compounded for, under certain circumstances, at a fixed penalty, and every portion of the body injured had its price, from the leg to the little finger, even down to the hair, tooth, or nail. The loss of an eye and a leg appears to have been considered the most important, and was punished by a fine of fifty shillings. To lame a person only, the sum exacted was thirty shillings. To wound, or strike such a blow as caused deafness, twenty-five shillings; for fracturing the skull, twenty shillings; for cutting off the little finger, eleven shillings; tearing off the hair, ten shillings. For tearing off a nail, or driving out a tooth, the penalty was one shilling; but if a front tooth, the charge was six shillings.

Robbery was punished according to the rank of the party plundered. If a freeman committed robbery, he forfeited all his goods and his freedom; if he was taken in the act, and the stolen property found in his hand, the king had the option of killing him, of selling him, or receiving the value of his Were, which was the sum at which his life would have been rated had he been murdered.

Even the life of the king had its Were or value. One hundred and twenty pounds was the price fixed to be paid as the penalty for the murder of a king. Taking the life of a noble, a bishop, an alderman, a thane, a servant, had each its fixed penalty, according to the rank of the deceased – from that of the king, as above named, to the humblest hind, whose life was rated at thirty shillings.

Besides the Were, there was another protection, called the Mund. This seems to have been a penalty paid for disturbing the peace of a man's household; or, as Sharon Turner has observed, "it was a privilege which made every man's house his castle."

The Saxons had also their bail or sureties. Thus, when a man had committed homicide, he had to find borh, or sureties for the payment of the penalty. The time allowed for payment is not mentioned, excepting in one case, where it appears to have been limited to 40 days.

The head of every tithing, or ten families, also appears to have been responsible for those under his jurisdiction or keeping, as we have previously shown in the reign of Alfred. He who had no surety, or borh, or could not pay the penalty for the crime committed, or had no kinsman to redeem him, either became a slave, or might be slain, depending on the nature of the offence.

Their mode of trial was very simple, and their general method of arriving at the innocence or guilt of the party accused appears to have been influenced by the number and respectability of the witnesses who swore for or against the prisoner.

Thus, if a man stood charged with any offence, and he could bring the required number of persons to swear that he was innocent, he would be acquitted, unless the accusing party could produce a greater number of witnesses to swear against him, and show clearer proofs of his guilt. When this was the case, the offender either submitted to the punishment or underwent the trial of ordeal, or, as it was considered, submitted to the 'judgment of God.'

The ordeal consisted either of hot water or hot iron; in some cases the iron weighed three pounds, and was to be carried nine paces. The ordeal appears to have taken place in the church; if the trial was to be by hot iron, a number of men were allowed to enter the church, and, being ranged on each side, the priest sprinkled them with holy water; they were then to kiss the Gospel, and were

signed with the cross. The priest afterwards read a prayer, and during this period the fire was not to be attended, and if burnt out the iron still rested upon the staples to cool, so that in no instance could it be red-hot. The paces were measured by the feet of the accused, and it has been computed that the hot iron would hardly remain in his hand beyond two seconds. Whether the culprit moved rapidly or walked slowly, or threw the iron upon the floor, or placed it on some allotted spot, we cannot tell; though there is but little doubt that means were taken to render the trial as short as possible.

When the ordeal was by water, it was sufficient if four witnesses stepped forward to state that they had seen it boiling; whether the vessel was of iron, copper, or clay, a stone was placed in it, which the accused with his bare hand and arm had to take out; the vessel was shallow or deep, according to the nature of the offence he stood charged with; in some cases he had only to plunge in his hand to take out the stone, in others he had to submerge his arm up to the elbow.

As in the ordeal by heated iron, the same ceremonies were observed, and during the time that elapsed in praying and sprinkling the witnesses, the fire was not allowed to be mended. While the act took place, a prayer was offered up to God to discover the truth.

When the trial was over, the hand or arm was bound up, and the bandages were not removed until three days had passed. It does not appear that the marks of burning or scalding were the tests of guilt; it was only when the wounds were found foul and unhealed that the accused was pronounced guilty; if they looked healthy and well, and were nearly healed, it was considered a proof of innocence.

It can easily be imagined that few who were guilty would willingly undergo such a trial, for it must be borne in mind that punishment still followed; and when the signs were unfavourable, there can be little doubt after so solemn a ceremony that the penalty the accused was doomed to suffer must have been severe.

It could, however, like homicide, be compounded for; and capital punishment seems seldom to have taken place amongst the Saxons, unless the crime was committed in broad daylight, and the culprit was caught in the act, or under such circumstances as were considered too clear to need any trial; in such cases, vengeance was sometimes taken on the spot, and the robber or murderer was either hanged upon the nearest tree, or slain where he was captured – no evidence was required, no defence was allowed.

There were two other forms of ordeal, called 'the cross' and 'the corsned'.

The cross consisted of two pieces of wood, which were covered over, one bearing the mark of the cross; if the accused drew this, he was considered innocent; if the piece was unmarked, the accused was guilty.

The corsned consisted of swallowing a piece of bread which the priest had blessed; if it stuck in the throat, or the culprit turned pale or trembled, or had difficulty swallowing it, his guilt was proven.

Besides fines, many of the punishments that were inflicted were severe; they used the whip and the heated brand, mutilated the face, they imprisoned, banished, sentenced the guilty to slavery, or doomed them to suffer imprisonment, while their capital punishments appear to have involved hanging and stoning to death.

The land was divided into what was called folkland and bocland. The folkland was such as belonged to the king and the people. That which was held by agreement or charter was called bocland, or land made over by agreement of the book, or some written instrument, though conveyances of land were sometimes made by the delivery of an arrow, a spear, or any other object.

The king had, however, his bocland or private property, as is proved by the will of king Alfred; and the word folkland in time was changed to 'crown land', which, no doubt, means that the wastes and commons which the people were allowed to make use of, and were not private property, were considered to belong to the king or the state.

Boclands appear originally to have been granted for only the lifetime of the holder. It was only over time, and in the course of events, that they became hereditary.

The Saxons were divided into many classes or ranks; first stood the king, then the earls, nobles, or chiefs; then came the other class of small landed proprietors; and below these another grade, whom we may call freemen; and then the theows, ceorls, or villains, came last, and were slaves of the soil.

If the estate changed hands, the theow went to the next owner; on no account could he leave the land; he was, however, protected, and, so long as he did his duty, could not be removed by the owner; neither could more than a regular portion of labour be demanded of him; and we have before alluded to his privileges in the laws of Ina.

The ceremonies used at their witenagemotes, guilds, moots, and other courts, are matters of law rather than subjects suited to a merely narrative and picturesque history of England.

LITERATURE

We have no proof that the early pagan Saxons possessed an alphabet, or had any acquaintance with a written language, until the introduction of Christianity; for, unlike the Britons, they had not the Romans to instruct them.

Even as late as Alfred's time, we have shown that only very few English chiefs could either read or write; and we find that Wihtred, king of Kent, as long after the Saxon invasion as the year 700, was unable to affix his signature to a charter, but instead directed a scribe (who had probably drawn up the document) to add as an explanation to the royal mark, that

> "I, Wihtred, king of Kent, have put this sign of the holy cross to the charter, on account of my ignorance of writing."

As the Saxons were the avowed enemies of the ancient Cymry, and came amongst them only to slay, destroy, and take possession of the land, it is easy to account for the length of time that must have elapsed before the Britons would impart the knowledge they had gathered from the Romans to their Saxon conquerors.

One of the earliest histories we possess is that to which the name of Gildas is affixed – who appears, however, to have belonged to the Cymry, and to have had a brother at that period who was celebrated as one of the Welsh bards. To him we have already referred; also to Nennius, who is said to have been one of the monks of Bangor, and to have had a narrow escape from the massacre in which so many of his brethren perished. To his early history of Britain we have before alluded.

Columbanus, a celebrated Irishman, who died in Italy about the year 615, appears to have been well acquainted with both the Greek and Hebrew languages. Literature at this period seems to have been confined principally to the monasteries; and towards the close of the sixth century, we find Aldhelm, an abbot of Malmsbury, celebrated for his Latin writings.

Sharon Turner says:

> "But his meaning is clouded by gorgeous rhetoric: his style an endless tissue of figures, which he never leaves till he has converted every metaphor into a simile, and every simile into a wearisome episode."

But the venerable Bede's is the most distinguished name amongst the early Anglo-Saxon writers. He also wrote in Latin, and his ecclesiastical history of England still stands as the chief authority from which we can derive the clearest knowledge of the manners and customs of the early Anglo-Saxons.

Bede was born about 670, or 680, at a village named Yarrow, which stands near the mouth of the Tyne, and was educated at the neighbouring monastery of Wearmouth. He was acquainted with Egbert, the learned archbishop of York, to whom he addressed a letter, which still extists. Egbert left behind him a famous library, mention of which is made by the celebrated Alcuin, who proposed to Charlemagne that the boys he was educating should be sent out of France, to

"...copy and carry back the flowers of Britain, that the garden might not be shut up in York, but the fruits of it placed in the paradise of Tours."

Though both writing in the same language, and during the same period, no two authors out of the thousands who have since lived and written, have ever exhibited a greater contrast in the style of composition than that which exists between the writings of Aldhelm and Bede.

> "The style of Bede," says Turner, "in all his works, is plain and unaffected. Attentive only to his matter, he had little solicitude for the phrase in which he dressed it; but, though seldom eloquent, and often homely, it is clear, precise, and useful."

Alfred was the first who translated the works of Bede into Saxon, and made them familiar to his subjects.

Alcuin, who speaks so highly of the library collected at York by the archbishop Egbert, was sent on an embassy by Offa, surnamed the Terrible, to Charlemagne. Alcuin was a pupil of Bede's, and a native of Northumbria; and while he was in France, he was instrumental in persuading the emperor to gather together many valuable manuscripts. His works seem to have been written for the use and instruction of his friend and  patron, the emperor Charlemagne – but, though highly valuable in their day, they lack that living spirit which was infused into the writings of Bede.

Few of the civilized nations of Europe possess works that bear comparison with those produced by our early Saxon writers; nor do any of the other Gothic tribes, from which our old Germanic language sprung, possess a literature of so old a date, that in any way approaches that attained by the early Anglo-Saxons. What we possess is unique, considering the short time that elapsed from the first introduction of letters amongst the Saxons, to the troubles which followed the Danish invasion, when so many monasteries and libraries were destroyed.

The first business of the Saxons, after they had ceased fighting and settled down in England, would be to build and plant; and much time and labour would be required in erecting their houses, preparing a supply of food, and defending their possessions in a new and hostile country, before they would be able to have sufficient leisure to direct their thoughts to literature, or indeed do anything more than establish those civil institutions which were necessary for the protection of the colony.

They had that work to do which we find ready done to our own hands; fields to inclose, and roads to make; and even the monks to whom we are indebted for our earliest writings were at first compelled to assist in building the monasteries they wrote in, and to cultivate the waste lands which lay around them.

And yet, in spite of these drawbacks, what wonderful progress was made in literature by the close of the reign of Alfred! Though illiterate, the early Saxons were a highly intelligent race: look at the speech of the chieftain we have already quoted in the reign of Edwin, the king of Deiri – the beautiful and applicable imagery of the bird, the warm hall it enters in winter, and the cold and darkness, which is compared to death, that reigns without; all evince a fine appreciation of the true elements which constitute poetry; and yet there is no doubt that the orator could neither read nor write.

When the Saxons turned their attention to letters, none of the surrounding illiterate nations excelled them – the progress made during the reign of Alfred was unique.

Nothing can be more primitive than our Anglo-Saxon poetry. Every line bears the stamp of originality. The praise of brave warriors is always the subject. It has always been the same. They

extolled what then stood highest in their estimation – the brave warrior, the giver of rewards, the terror of enemies, the leader of battles. The poems are the plaudits put into metre, the natural outbreak of admiration.

Watch a fond mother when alone, talking to her infant. Nature is still the same – she addresses it as her darling, her dearest, her life, her delight; and when she has exhausted every endearing epithet, and uttered every fond word there is, she evinces her affection by caresses. To what lengths could we extend the comparison!

But neither mother nor child in those days earned the lavish praises which were expended on a brave chieftain. We need only refer to the extracts we have already given in the body of our history, from the Welsh bards, to show this.

The literature in no country was ever built upon such an original foundation as that of the Anglo-Saxons. Their language at an early period had been enriched by the Danish: their habits resembled those of the sea-kings.

Long before the Norman conquest, the two groups had melded into one; the sea-horses, and the road of the swans, were to them familiar images; there was a sublimity about the ocean, and the storm, and the giant headlands, which the Saxons felt and understood; and had we the space, we could fill pages with proofs of this grand poetical appreciation, with its natural inspiration.

The Saxon ode which celebrates Athelstan's victory at Brunanburg bears evidence of the fiery spirit which the Scandinavians diffused. Neither drew from the classic stores of Rome or Greece; this blend is a northern creation.

    Their homilies and graver works scarcely come within the compass of our history; they require more serious treatment than we are able to bestow upon them. Those attributed to Alfric are now on the eve of becoming widely known; and there is no doubt that in the course of time, the study of the Anglo-Saxon language will be pursued by every person who aspires to literature.

    A few days' attention to it renders the reading of Chaucer easy; and although it will take time before students are able to decypher an old Saxon manuscript, yet they will be rewarded by the facility with which they will get through our early stores of black-letter lore.

    Ballads were sung in the English streets before the time of Alfred. Our music and singing-parties are nothing new. More than a thousand years ago, the harp sounded in the festal hall, accompanied by the voice of the singer. Look at the beauty of the following extract.

It is an old Saxon song, and was known long before the Normans invaded England. The exile is banished from his friends, and encounters many hardships. He is doomed to dwell in a cave within the forest; and thus he complains:

> This earthly dwelling is cold, and I am weary;
> The mountains are high up, the dells are gloomy,
> Their streets full of branches, roofed with pointed thorns;
> I am weary of so cheerless an abode.
> My friends are now all in the earth –
> The grave guards all that I loved;
> I alone remain above, and thitherward am I going.
> All the long summer day I sit weeping
> Under the oak tree, near my earthly cave,
> And there may I long weep.
> The exile's path still lies through a land of troubles;
> My mind knows no rest – it is the cave of care.
> Throughout life has weariness ever pursued me.

This passage wants but the polish of Shakespeare, and to be uttered by his own mournful monarch, King Richard the Second.

ARCHITECTURE, ART, AND SCIENCE

That the Saxons possessed considerable skill in architecture before they took possession of England, we have already shown in our description of the pagan temple which was erected in their own country. It is also on record that the Christian missionaries sent over by Pope Gregory converted the heathen temples, which they found already erected in our island, into churches, destroying only the idols they found therein; but whether these edifices were erected by the Britons or Romans, or by the Saxons themselves, it is difficult to decide. All we know for a certainty is that the church in which Augustine and his monks were located on their arrival at Canterbury was called an ancient British temple, and was probably built by the first Christians who were converted by the Romans.

The earliest churches which the Saxons erected after their conversion to Christianity were formed of wood, and covered with thatch; and even as late as the time of Chaucer, we find mention of the sacred edifices being roofed with the same substance.

The celebrated cathedral of Lindisfarne could boast of no costlier material than sawn oak and a straw roof, until Eadbert, the seventh bishop, removed the thatch, and threw over the rafters a covering of lead.

The minster of York, founded by Edwin, after his marriage with Edilburga, the daughter of Ethelbert, was built of stone; and as early as 669, we find mention of the windows being glazed. Prior to this period, the windows consisted of mere openings in the walls, through which the light was admitted; they were called eye-holes, and were protected by lattice-work, through which the birds flew in and out, and built inside the fabric; nor was there any other means of keeping out the rain and snow, excepting by lowering down the simple linen blinds.

The few examples we possess today of Saxon architecture display great strength and solidity, and are largely without grace. The columns are low and massy, the arches round and heavy,

seeming as if they formed a portion of the bulky pillars, instead of springing from them with that light and airy grace which is the great beauty of Gothic architecture.

Their chief ornament in building appears to have been the zig-zag moulding which resembles sharks' teeth. The very word they used in describing this form of ornament also signified to gnaw or eat; and from the Saxon word fret, or teeth work, the common term of fret-work arose.

Towards the close of the seventh century, the celebrated bishop Wilfrid, who had visited Rome, made great improvements in ecclesiastical architecture. He brought with him several eminent artists from Italy; and as he stood high in the favour of Oswy, king of the Deiri and Bernicia, he was able to reward his architects liberally.

He restored the church which Paulinus founded at York. But the most celebrated edifice he raised appears to have been the church at Hexham, of which the following description is given by Richard, who was the prior of Hexham, and who wrote while the building still existed about the close of the twelfth century:

> "The foundations of this church were laid deep in the earth for the crypts and oratories, and the passages leading to them, which were then with great exactness contrived and built under ground.

The walls, which were of great length, and raised to an immense height, and divided into three several stories, or tiers, he (Wilfrid) supported by square and various other kinds of well-polished columns. Also, the walls, the capitals of the columns which supported them, and the arch of the sanctuary, he decorated with historical representations, imagery, and various figures in relief, carved in stone, and painted with a variety of colours.

The body of the church is compassed about with pentices and porticoes, which, both above and below, are divided, with great and inexpressible art, by partition walls and winding stairs.

Within the staircases, and above them, are flights of steps and galleries of stone, and several passages leading from them, both ascending and descending, to be artfully disposed, so that multitudes of people might be there, and go quite round the church, without being seen by any one below in the nave."

Prior Richard goes on further to state, that he also caused several altars to be erected to the blessed saints. In 767, the church of St. Peter's at York having been either damaged or destroyed by fire, was rebuilt by archbishop Albert, assisted by the celebrated Alcuin, who we have already mentioned.

Here, also, we find mention of lofty arches, supported on columns, of vaultings, windows, porticoes, galleries, and altars, richly ornamented.

What additions the genius of Alfred made to the architecture of the period we do not know. We have, however, already shown that he set apart a great portion of his revenue to the building and

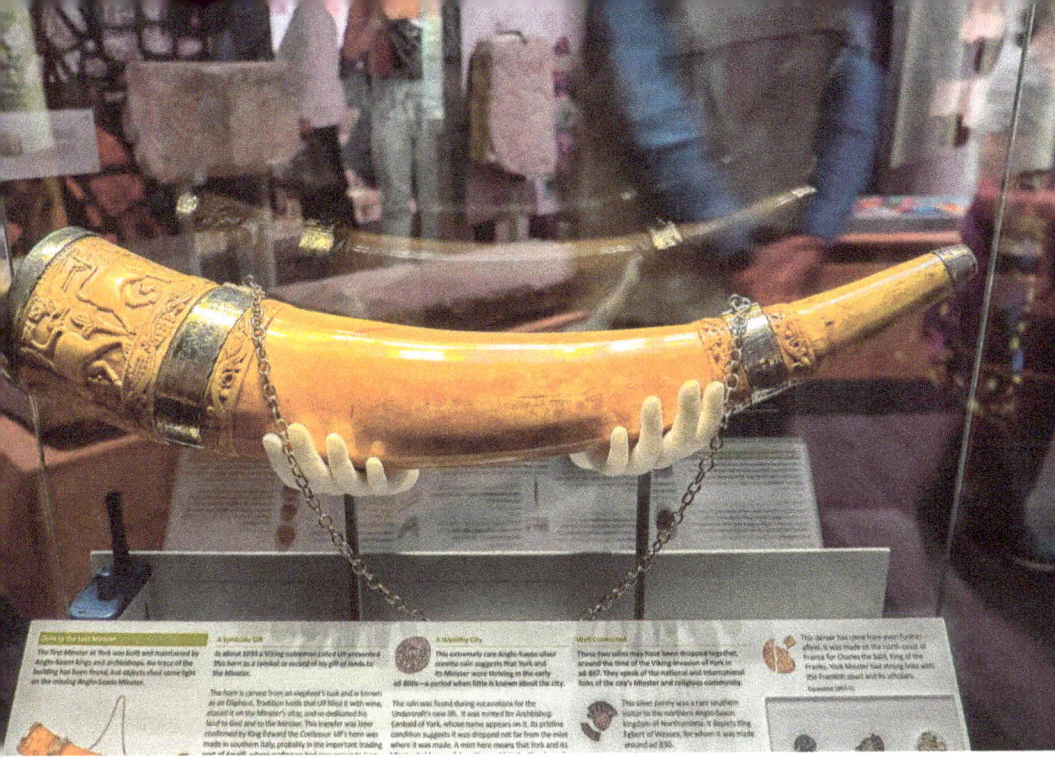

repairing of churches. But he lived amid stormy times, when the strengthening of military fortresses was of more consequence to the welfare of his kingdom than the erection of costly edifices; and during the ravages of the Danes, the fine arts appear not to have made any advance.

We have scarcely any records of the domestic architecture of the Saxons, but may safely infer, from the simple style of their early churches, that their houses were built of wood, and thatched with reeds, and we have proof that timber houses continued until a comparatively modern period.

*

Of their painting and sculpture we know only little.

The horn of Ulphus (above), which is still preserved, is beautifully carved; and we find mention of the tomb of the bishop of Hexham having been richly decorated. Their paintings seem to have been imported from Rome, and were principally pictures of saints and martyrs, which appear to have formed the most attractive ornaments in their churches. Their illuminated missals we have already alluded to.

The Saxon women were skilful embroiderers, weavers, and spinners, arts in which the daughters of Edward the Elder excelled. Even the celebrated St. Dunstan, with all his surliness, deigned to draw patterns for his fair countrywomen to copy in their embroidery.

Among other costly gifts, mentioned in a Charter relating to Croyland Abbey, granted by a king of Mercia, we find a golden veil, on which was enwrought the famous siege of Troy. Many of the initial letters, already mentioned, are of the most intricate patterns, scroll is interlaced within scroll, chain-like links, and heads of birds and serpents, running into the most beautiful flourishes, and compelling us to admit that the Saxons were either excellent copyists, or gifted with considerable invention.

*

Their musical instruments consisted of horns, trumpets, flutes, drums, cymbals, a stringed instrument not unlike the violin, which was played upon with a bow, and the harp; and in their churches organs which must have shaken the sacred buildings with their powerful tones.

Dunstan was celebrated for his skill on the harp; he also made an organ with brass pipes, and made several presents of bells to the Saxon churches.

From the description given of a harp in an old poem, it was made of birch-wood, with oaken keys, and strung with the long hairs pulled from the tails of horses.

The cymbals were formed of mixed metals, and were struck on the concave side, as they are now; and Bede dwells upon their beautiful modulation in the hands of a skilful player.

He describes the drum as having been made of stretched leather, fastened on rounded hoops, and which emitted a loud sound when struck – he mentions tones, and semi-tones, and says of the power of music:

> "Among all the sciences this is the more commendable, pleasing, courtly, mirthful, and lovely. It makes men liberal, cheerful, courteous, glad, and amiable – it rouses them to battle – it exhorts them to bear fatigue, and comforts them under labour: it refreshes the mind that is disturbed, chases away headache and sorrow, dispels the depraved humours, and cheers the desponding spirits."

We find the Saxon organs described as rising high, some having gilded pipes, and many pairs of bellows; one especially is pointed out by the monk Wolfstan, as having stood in Winchester cathedral: "Such a one had never before been seen."

Sharon Turner says:

> "It seems to have been a prodigious instrument. It had twelve bellows above, and fourteen below, which were alternately worked by seventy strong men, covered with perspiration, and emulously animating each other to impel the blast with all their strength.
>
> There were four hundred pipes, which the hand of the skilful organist shut or opened as the tune required. Two friars sat at it, whom a rector governed. It had concealed holes adopted to forty keys; they struck the seven notes of the octave, the carmine of the lyric semi-tone being mixed.
>
> It must have reached the full sublime of musical sound, so far as its quantity produces sublimity."

*

In arithmetic, they simply studied the division of even numbers, separating them into those "metaphysical distinctions of equally equal, and equally unequal," though they seem to have attained something approaching to perfection in calculation.

In natural philosophy, Bede was far in advance of many of the Roman writers. In astronomy, they drew their information from such Greek and Latin treatises as chanced to fall into their hands. They believed that comets portended war, pestilence, and famine, and all those evils which the ignorant still attribute to their appearance in the present day.

Of geography they knew but little, until the work of Orosius was translated by our own Alfred.

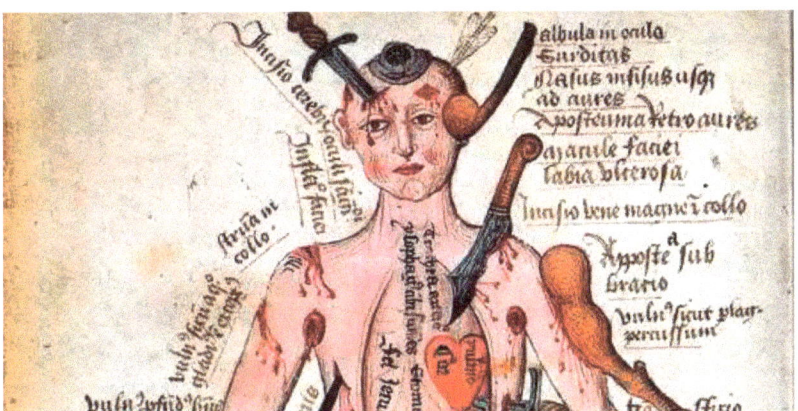

They sought to cure diseases by charms, though they were not without physicians, herbs being what they principally used for medicine; and, no doubt, many of our village herb-doctors, who trust to the full or wane of the moon, for finding the healing virtues in their favourite plants, are fair samples of the early Saxon practitioner in the same art.

Many old books, such as *The Gentlewoman's Closet,* contain the genuine recipes used by the Saxons. From a rare original work, in our possession, we quote the following, whose counterpart may be found in many a valuable Saxon recipe:

> "The sixth and tenth days of March shalt thou draw
> out blood of the right arm, the eleventh day of
> April, and in the end of May, of which arm thou
> wilt, and that against a fever; and if thou dost,
> neither shalt thou lose thy sight, nor thou shalt
> have no fever so long as thou livest!"

He who fell sick on the first day of the month, was supposed to be in danger for three days after; on the second day, would get well; on the third, was to be ill for 28 days; on the fourth, to escape; on the fifth, to suffer grievously; and on the eighth,

"...if he be not whole on the twelfth day, he shall be dead."

And so on, for every day throughout the month and year.

COSTUME, MANNERS, CUSTOMS, AND EVERYDAY LIFE

Of the every-day life and domestic manners of our Anglo-Saxon forefathers, we possess considerable information, partly from written records, such as charters, wills, grants, and leases, but more especially from the drawings which we find in the ancient manuscripts which are still preserved.

Amongst the higher classes, we discover that the walls were hung with tapestry, ornamented with gold and rich colours, for the needles of the Saxon ladies seem ever to have been employed in forming birds, animals, trees, and flowers, upon the hangings which were so necessary to keep out the wind that must have blown in at every chink of their wooden apartments.

*

Their garments were loose and flowing. Mens' clothing consisted of a shirt, over which they wore a coat or tunic, open at the neck and partly up the sides, having wide sleeves which reached to the wrists; and as this was ample enough to be put on by slipping it over the head, (not unlike the common frock worn by our carters or peasantry,) it was occasionally, and no doubt always in cold weather, to make it sit closer, confined to the waist by a girdle or belt.

Over this they occasionally wore a short cloak, which was fastened to the breast by a brooch or loop; they also wore drawers or long hose, which were bandaged crosswise, from the ankle to the knee, with strips of coloured cloth or leather.

Their shoes, which were open at the front, were secured by thongs; and though the poorer classes are sometimes represented as bare-legged, yet they are seldom drawn without shoes, which are generally painted black, while many of them wear the short stocking or sock.

That their shoes were made of leather is expressly stated by Bede, who describes St. Cuthbert, as often keeping on his shoes for months together, and that it was with difficulty he could be persuaded to take them off, to permit his feet to be made clean.

Hats or caps they seem rarely to have worn, although there are one or two instances in which they appear. They seem generally to have gone bareheaded, excepting when in battle; then they wore a pointed helmet.

In nearly all the early illustrations, we find the hair worn long, parted in the middle, and falling down upon the neck and shoulders. The beard is also long and forked.

Silk garments were not uncommon amongst the nobles: as early as the time of Ethelbert, king of Kent, mention is made of a silk dress. We also read of a coronation garment, which was made of silk, and woven of gold and flowers. In the churches the altars were generally covered with silk, and at his death, the body of the venerable Bede was enclosed in a silken shroud.

The Saxon noblemen seem to have been lavish in their ornaments, and to have worn costly bracelets on their arms, and rings upon their fingers – the ring appears to have been worn upon the third finger of the right hand – it was called the gold finger, and the penalty for cutting this off was greater than for amputating any of the other fingers.

Furs of sable, beaver, fox, martin and other animals were also worn, and amongst the poorer classes the skins of lambs and sheep were worn.

The costume of the Saxon ladies seems to have varied only little, excepting in length, from that worn by the men.

The gunna, or gown, which was worn over the skirt or kirtle, was of the same form as the tunic already described; it was a little shorter than the kirtle, which reached to the feet – the latter being covered by shoes similar to those already mentioned.

The women, however, wore a head-dress, formed of linen or silk, which looks not unlike the hood of comparatively modern times. It was called the head-rail, and besides forming a covering for the head, was made to enfold the neck and shoulders, not unlike the gorget which we see in ancient armour, in appearance; but formed by throwing fold over fold – making the face appear as if it looked out from a close-fitting helmet or gorget.

Nor were the Saxon ladies at all deficient in ornaments. They had their cuffs and ribbons, necklaces and bracelets, ear-rings and brooches, set with gems. They were adept at twisting and curling the hair; and they also painted their cheeks, so that England has long had its rouged, as well as its rosy daughters.

We read also of pale tunics, of dun-coloured garments, of white kirtles – and, in the Anglo-Saxon illustrations, we see robes of purple bordered with yellow, of green striped with red, of lilac interlaced with green, crimson striped with purple, all showing that a love of rich and pleasing colours was, above a thousand years ago, common to the ladies of England.

Gloves appear to have been rarely worn. The sleeve of the tunic was made long enough to be drawn over the hand in cold weather; where the glove is represented, the thumb only is separate, the remainder of the fingers are covered, without any division, like the mits, or mittens, worn by children at the present day.

*

The military costume we have already described: nor does it appear to have undergone any alteration until after the Norman Conquest. They wore helmets, had wooden shields covered with leather, rimmed, and bossed with iron, had a kind of ringed armour to defend the breast, and such weapons as we have frequently made mention of in our descriptions of the battles.

*

Turning to their furniture, we find, that besides benches and stools, they had also seats with backs to them, not unlike the chairs or sofas of the present day. Many of these are richly ornamented with the forms of lions, eagles, and dragons; and no better proof need be advanced than this profusion of carved work, to show that in their domestic comforts they had stepped far beyond the mere wants and common necessaries of life, and made considerable progress in its refinements and luxuries.

Their chairs and tables were not only formed of wood richly carved, but sometimes inlaid with gold, silver, and ivory.

Nor were the eating and drinking vessels of the nobles less costly. Mention is made of gold and silver cups, on which figures of men and animals were engraven; and the weight of some of these was from two to four pounds.

They covered their tables with cloths; had knives, spoons, drinking-horns, bowls, dishes, but in no instance do we see a fork. The roast meat or fowl appears to have been served on long spits; each guest cut off what he wanted, and then the attendant passed on to the next, who also helped himself. The bread and salt stood ready for all upon the table.

The Saxons were hard drinkers – mead, wine, and ale flowed freely at their feasts; and it seems to have been a common custom for the guests to have slept in the apartment where the feast was held; for we read of the tables being removed, of bolsters being brought into the hall, and the company throwing themselves upon the floor, their only covering being their cloaks or skins, while their weapons were suspended from the boarded walls over their heads.

Bedsteads were, however, in use, though they appear to have been low; the part where the head rested was raised like the end of a modern couch; beds, pillows, bed-clothes, curtains, sheets, and coverlets of linen and skins, are occasionally mentioned in the old

Saxon wills, where we also find both the words sacking (coarse cloth) and bolster (cushion). The bed-pillows appear occasionally to have been made of plaited straw; and in one place we find mention of bed-curtains formed of gilded fly-net, but what this may have been, we do not know.

We read also of candlesticks, hand-bells, and mirrors being made of silver.

Glass appears to have been used more sparingly, though it is mentioned by Bede as being used for lamps and vessels. The use of the bath is also frequently named; and we find them using frankincense, pepper, and cinnamon, and other spices.

*

England at this time abounded in woods, and the chief meat of the Saxons appears to have been the flesh of swine. Pigs are frequently mentioned in wills. They were given in dowries, bequeathed to abbeys and monasteries, together with the land on which the swine fed. Oxen and sheep they used more sparingly; and it is very probable that they were not, during this period, as plentiful as pigs.

Deer, goats, and hares, and several varieties of fowl, were also used for food.

Of fish, the eel appears to have been the most abundant. Eels were often received in payment of rent; estates were held by no other form than that of presenting so many eels annually; and eel-dykes are mentioned as forming the boundary lines of different possessions. Herrings, salmon, sturgeons, flounders, plaice, crabs, lobsters, oysters, muscles, cockles, winkles, and even the porpoise, are named amongst the fish which they consumed.

Cheese, milk, butter, and eggs were among the staple foods of the Saxons. They used also both wheat and barley bread, and had wind and water mills to grind their corn.

They appear to have been great consumers of honey; and amongst their vegetables, beans and colewort are frequently mentioned. In their soups they used herbs; and amongst their fruits we find pears, apples, grapes, nuts, and even almonds and figs were grown in the orchards which belonged to the monasteries.

Salt was extensively used; and they seem to have slaughtered numbers of their cattle in autumn, which they cured and salted for winter consumption; and from this we might infer that there was a scarcity of fodder during the winter months.

They boiled, baked, and roasted their food as we do now. Mention is made of their ovens and boiling vessels, and of their fish having been broiled. To eat or drink what a cat or dog had spoiled, they were compelled afterwards to undergo a penance; also, if anyone gave to another any liquor in which a mouse or a weazel had been found dead, four days' penance was inflicted; or if a monk, he was doomed to sing three hundred psalms.

There seem to have been ale-houses or taverns at a very early period; and we find a priest forbidden to either eat or drink in those places where ale was sold.

So plentiful does animal food appear to have been, that a master was prohibited from giving it to his servants on fast-days; if he did, he was sentenced to the pillory.

*

 Beginning with their in-door sports and pastimes, we find games similar to chess and backgammon amongst their social amusements, while gleemen, dancers, tumblers, and harpers all contributed to their merriment.

In the early illuminations, we see jugglers throwing up three knives and balls, and catching each alternately, just as the same feat is performed in the present day.

The Saxons were also great lovers of the chase. Alfred, as we have shown, was a famous hunter; and Harold received his surname of Harefoot through his swiftness in following the chase. Boars and wild deer appear to have been their favourite game, and sometimes they hunted down grey wolves. Wolf-traps and wolf-pits are often mentioned in the Saxon records.

England was not in those days cursed with game laws. Every man might pursue the game upon his own land, and over hundreds of miles of wood and moor-hill, dale and common, without any one interfering with him.

There was no exception made, only to the spot in which the king hunted, and this restriction appears only to have been limited to the time and place where he followed the chase. When the royal hunt was over, the forest was again free. The Saxons hunted with hawks and hounds; and Alfred the Great wrote instructions on the management of hawks. Nets, pits, bows and arrows, and slings, were also used for capturing and destroying game.

*

Women were protected by many excellent laws; and violence offered to them was visited by such severe pains and penalties as to make us ashamed of the justice which the insulted female obtains in modern times when she seeks redress.

The first step towards marriage consisted in obtaining the lady's consent, the second that of her parents or friends; the intended husband then pledged himself to maintain his wife in becoming dignity; his friends were bound for the fulfilment of his engagement.

Next, provision was made for the children; and here, again, the husband had to find sureties. Then came the morgen-gift, or jointure, which was either money or land, paid or made over the day after the marriage.

Provision was also made in case of the husband's death, but if a widow married within twelve months of her widowhood, she forfeited all claim to the property of her former husband. The marriage ceremony was solemnized by the presence of the priest, who having consecrated their union, prayed for the Divine blessing to settle upon them, and that they might live in holiness, happiness, and prosperity.

Women had property in their own right, which they could dispose of without the husband's consent; they were also witnesses at the signing of deeds and charters.

In the Saxon manuscripts we never meet with the figures of women engaged in out-of-door labour; this was always done by the men, although the wealthy classes had slaves of both sexes.

To women, the household occupation seems solely to have belonged. Alfred the Great wrote the following description of the love of a wife for her husband:

> "She lives now for thee, and thee only; hence she loves nothing else but thee. She has enough of every good in this present life, but she has despised it all for thee alone. She has shunned it all because she has not thee also. This one thing is now wanting to her; thine absence makes her think that all which she possesses is nothing. Hence, for thy love she is wasting; and full nigh dead with tears and sorrow."

Who can doubt but that this passage describes his own feelings, when he wandered hungry and homeless about the wilds of Athelney, and thought of her he had left weeping in solitude behind? It is one of the many original passages which are found in his Boethius, for Alfred was no mere translator, but enriched his author from the storehouse of his own thoughts.

*

When they were pagans, the Saxons frequently burnt the bodies of their dead, but they abandoned this custom when they converted to Christianity.

Their first mode of interment appears to have been a grave, in which they placed the body without any covering excepting the earth which was thrown over it. Sometimes the body was rolled in a sheet of lead; and at Swinehead's Abbey, in Lincolnshire, several skeletons have been dug up lately, wrapped round with the same material, but without any vestige of a coffin appearing; though this is no proof of wooden coffins not having been used at the period of interment, which through the lapse of long centuries may have decayed and mingled with the soil.

Stone coffins were commonly used by the wealthy, and but few were at first allowed to be buried within walled towns. By degrees the churches began to be used as places of burial, though only men distinguished for their piety and good works appear at first to have been buried in these ancient edifices.

After a time, the churches and church-yards became crowded with graves, and then the bodies were removed to some distance for burial. The passing-bell was rung at a very early period; it is mentioned by Bede, and there is little doubt that the custom dates from nearly the first introduction of Christianity.

The clergy, on the death of a person, received a payment, called the *soul-scot*, which could amount to an immense sum; even land was left by the dead, that prayers might be offered up for the welfare of the soul; thus in early times the churches were made rich.

The burial of Archbishop Wilfred, in the eighth century, is described by Eddius:

> "Upon a certain day, many abbots and clergy met those who conducted the corpse of the holy bishop in a hearse, and begged that they might be permitted to wash the body, and dress it honourably, as befitted its dignity.
>
> This was granted; and an abbot named Baculus then spread his surplice on the ground, and the brethren depositing the body upon it, washed it with their own hands, then, dressing it in the ecclesiastical habit, they carried it along, singing psalms and hymns as they proceeded.
>
> When they approached the monastery, the monks came out to meet it, and scarcely one refrained from shedding tears and weeping aloud. And thus the body was borne, amid hymns and tears, to its final resting-place – the church which the good bishop had built and dedicated to Saint Peter."

The Saxons had also guilds or clubs, in which the artisans, or such as seem to have consisted of the middle classes, subscribed for the burial of a member, and a fine was inflicted upon every brother who did not attend the funeral.

Thus, more than a thousand years ago, were burial societies established in England – a clear proof of the respect which Saxons had for their dead.

A DISTANT MIRROR

Béchamp or Pasteur?
Ethel Hume

The Blood and its Third Element
Antoine Béchamp

Reconstruction by Way of the Soil
The Wheel of Health
Guy Wrench

The Soil and Health
Albert Howard

The Soul of the White Ant
The Soul of the Ape & My Friends the Baboons
Eugene Marais

The Day of the Nefilim
Air for Fire
David Major

Earthworm
George Oliver

My Inventions
The Problem of Increasing Human Energy
Nikola Tesla

Illuminati
Myron Fagan

Response in the Living and Non-living
Jagadish Bose

Ten Acres is Enough
Edmund Morris

ADISTANTMIRROR.COM

www.ingramcontent.com/pod-product-compliance
Lightning Source LLC
Chambersburg PA
CBHW051535010526
44107CB00064B/2733